CHRISTIAN CITIZENS IN AN ISLAMIC STATE

Christian Citizens in an Islamic State deals with the important question of inter-faith relations in Pakistan, a vital region of the Islamic world which has been the scene of the rise of both Islamic militancy and partnership with the West in counter-terrorism measures. Christians are the most important religious minority of Pakistan and their status and experience is a test case of the treatment of religious minorities in an Islamic state.

This book covers new ground in exploring the various factors that govern the relations between Muslims and Christians in a nation state which has been politically unstable in the past, and where the imposition of Islamic law has been controversial and problematic for religious minorities. Theodore Gabriel clarifies the history of Christian-Muslim relations in the region, explores the rise of Islamic militancy, and draws on personal interviews to determine the mind set of both Christians and Muslims in Pakistan today.

Christian Citizens in an Islamic State
The Pakistan Experience

THEODORE GABRIEL
University of Gloucestershire, UK

ASHGATE

Published by
Ashgate Publishing Limited
Gower House
Croft Road
Aldershot
Hampshire GU11 3HR
England

Ashgate Publishing Company
Suite 420
101 Cherry Street
Burlington, VT 05401-4405
USA

Ashgate website: http://www.ashgate.com

British Library Cataloguing in Publication Data
Gabriel, Theodore P. C.
  Christian citizens in an Islamic state : the Pakistan experience
  1. Christianity and other religions – Pakistan 2. Christianity and other religions – Islam
  3. Islam – Relations – Christianity 4. Christians – Pakistan – Social conditions
  I. Title
  297.2'83'095491

Library of Congress Cataloging-in-Publication Data
Gabriel, Theodore.
  Christian citizens in an islamic state : the Pakistan experience / Theodore Gabriel.
      p. cm.
  Includes bibliographical references.
  ISBN 978-0-7546-6024-8 (hardcover : alk. paper) – ISBN 978-0-7546-6036-1 (pbk. : alk. paper) 1. Christians–Pakistan. 2. Christianity and other religions–Pakistan. 3. Christianity and other religions–Islam. 4. Islam–Relations–Christianity. I. Title.

  BR1145.G33 2007
  297.2'83095491–dc22

                                                                                    2007022826

ISBN: 978-0-7546-6024-8 (Hbk)
ISBN: 978-0-7546-6036-1 (Pbk)

Printed and bound in Great Britain by TJ International Ltd, Padstow, Cornwall.

Contents

Foreword

The most significant feature of the religious situation in our time is the emergence of a post-Western Christianity and a post-Christian West. Over its first eight or nine centuries Christianity spread across much of the Eurasian landmass (the Emperor of China was first hearing Christian preaching at much the same time as the King of Northumbria) and into East Africa. But some centuries later Europe and "Christendom" (that is, Christianity) had become identified in the minds of Christians and Muslims alike. The identification powerfully influenced Christian and Muslim perceptions of each other, both in the long period of competition for territory between the peoples of Europe and their neighbours to the east and south, and in the period of Western colonial dominance over much of the non-Western world.

Today, however, the majority of Christians are Africans, Asians and Latin Americans, and the proportion they form of the total Christian community rises year on year. Christianity is now primarily a non-Western religion; its hold on the West, especially upon Europe, has long been slipping, but it has found new life and vigour in the non-Western world. This fact brings a wholly new element into Muslim-Christian relations, and gives added importance to such studies as Dr Gabriel has undertaken.

Dr Gabriel shows that Pakistan, the first modern Islamic state, was in its origins by no means an Islamist one. Christians readily identified with the new state, not seeking, as so many of their Hindu neighbours did, to migrate from it; they were not a conquered people, they were not *dhimmi*, they were citizens. Dr Gabriel describes the shifts in power and the changes in political structure since those days, with the religious, ethnic and ideological tensions that underlie them and the different traditions within Islam that they illustrate. He also reveals their effect on the small but significant Christian community of Pakistan. His verdict on the effect of the foreign policy of Western powers is trenchantly expressed; his account of the local efforts at building mutual understanding between Christians and Muslims is suffused with hope. And his concerned account of a Christian community in a changeable and changing Islamic context should inform and deepen awareness of the formative influence of religion in today's world; a world with a post-Christian West and a post-Western Christianity.

Andrew F. Walls
Centre for the Study of Christianity in the
Non-Western World, University of Edinburgh

Acknowledgements

I am grateful to the British Academy for the grant given to me that has made my research in Pakistan and this monograph possible. The authorities of the University of Gloucestershire and my colleagues, especially Dr Shelly Saguaro, Head of Department of Humanities, also cooperated fully with my enterprise and I acknowledge the facilities that they accorded in this connection with gratitude.

Professor Andrew F. Walls, Honorary Professor in Religious Studies at the University of Edinburgh, who kindly wrote the foreword to this book was my teacher at the University of Aberdeen and my mentor in the field of Religious Studies for over two decades. I owe him a debt of gratitude for his encouragement and unfailing help whenever asked for. He along with Professor Chris Partridge of the University of Lancaster also acted as referees for my application for a grant to the British Academy and I am grateful to them on this account.

I thank also the eminent personalities in Pakistan who gave me interviews in the middle of busy schedules and spoke candidly and informatively to me about Christian-Muslim relations in Pakistan and various relevant matters. Wherever I went the people I met in Pakistan – in universities, hotels, libraries etc. – were unstinting in their cooperation and good will and therefore I had a very enjoyable and productive time in that beautiful country. Therefore, though the present situation in Pakistan is far from being salutary, I am quite sanguine about its prosperous future.

I thank my colleague Dr Alison Scott-Baumann of the University of Gloucestershire for reading through my manuscript and for her helpful comments and suggestions.

I thank the editors of Ashgate and especially Ms Sarah Lloyd for accepting this monograph for publication.

Last but not least I acknowledge with thanks the help of Accompli for formatting the typescript.

Map of Pakistan

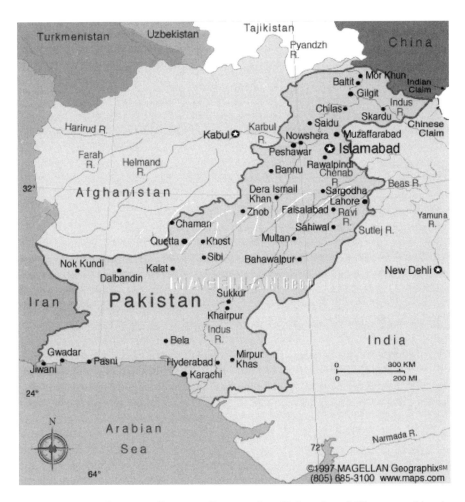

The assistance of Ms. Trudi James, Cartographer, University of Gloucestershire, in preparing this map is gratefully acknowledged.

Pakistan: Population by religion

	%		
	Muslim	Christian	Hindu
Pakistan	96.28	1.59	1.60
Panjab	97.21	2.31	0.13
Sindh	91.31	0.97	6.51
Balochistan	98.75	0.40	0.49
Islamabad	95.53	4.07	0.02

Chapter One

Introduction

The Islamic nation of Pakistan has a high profile in world politics. This is due to various reasons, both historical and contemporary. Pakistan came into prominence during the Indian independence movement, due to what is known as the two-nation theory. This doctrine, advanced by some of the leading Muslims of British India, averred that the Hindus and Muslims of India constituted two nations. It was Mohammed Iqbal, poet and philosopher, who first proposed the creation of a Muslim state to be carved out of British India. He did this in his chair's address at the Muslim League convention of 1930 and was critical of Muhammad Ali Jinnah, later to be known as Qaid I Azam (Father of the Nation) of Pakistan, and the first President of Pakistan. Iqbal stated:

> I would like to see the Panjab, NWFP, Sind and Balochistan amalgamated into a single state. Self government within the British Empire or without the British Empire, the formation of a consolidated North Western Indian Muslim state appears to me to be the final destiny of the Muslims, at least of North Western India[1]

Jinnah was a member of both the Indian National Congress and the Muslim League, and was a champion of Indian unity at that time and was not demanding the creation of a separate Muslim state in India. Jinnah was however concerned at the backwardness of the Muslim population of India, and in the Lucknow Pact of 1916 had received guarantees from the Congress that would avert the exploitation of Muslims by the more educationally advanced and numerically superior Hindu majority. However, the Nehru Report of 1928 undermined Jinnah's faith in Indian nationalism. The electoral system proposed in the report was certain to undermine the advantage of Muslim numerical superiority in Bengal and the Punjab since it was based on education and property ownership, in which the Muslims, though numerically superior, were backward, and the permanent Hindu authority in the centre had powers over the provinces. Moreover, the separate electorates guaranteed in the Lucknow pact were replaced in the Nehru report by joint electorates. Subsequently, the partial democratisation of India with elections to provincial governments in 1937 dealt another blow to Muslim hopes, when the Congress reneged on the commitment to form coalition ministries with the Muslim league. Jinnah's faith in Indian nationalism and unity were now completely undermined and he left the Indian National Congress. Jinnah seemed to find corroboration in these events of the basic communalism of the Congress, however strongly Gandhi and Nehru reiterated their commitment to

---

1   Ali, Chaudhuri, Muhammad, *The Emergence of Pakistan* (Lahore, 1986), pp. 23-4.

Indian inter-religious unity and the congress's impartiality. The division of India on the basis of religions had now become almost inevitable.

The ideology of Pakistan was nevertheless not one based on religion or Islam. It was a homeland for the Muslims of India, but in a political, not religious sense. I agree with Hamza Alawi that Islam was not at the heart of Muslim nationalism in British India.[2] Both Iqbal and Jinnah had emphasised many a time that Pakistan was not to be a theocratic state. The creation of Pakistan was based on a negative premise, namely to save the Muslim community of India from exploitation and discrimination by the Hindu majority. So it was the apparent attitude of Hindus that was the strongest factor, not Muslim identity or separatism, in the genesis of Pakistan. Some of the leaders of the Congress such as Vallabbhai Patel and Rajendra Prasad and many others had a background of Hindu-oriented organisations such as the Hindu Mahasabha and the RSS, though they all professed to be against communalism. While the impartiality of Gandhi and Nehru was above question, the religious neutrality of the Congress as a whole was not trusted by Muslim leaders such as Iqbal and Jinnah. Even the Mahatma with his use of Hindu symbols such as Rama Rajya and cow veneration, though perfectly innocent of any communalistic implications, was liable to misunderstanding and misinterpretation by Muslims.

Pakistan is also very much in the news in contemporary times due to its role in the ouster of the Soviets from Afghanistan, and its dispute with India on Kashmir. Its present support of the war on terror by President Bush has also pushed Pakistan into the limelight. Pakistan has, however, been and still is to a lesser extent the foremost breeding ground for Islamic militancy and training of *mujahideen* (Holy Warriors). This started during the period of opposition to Soviet hegemony in Afghanistan and was actively promoted by Pakistan under Zia ul Haqq, the foremost champion of Islamic fundamentalism among Pakistan's rulers, and also the USA, Saudi Arabia and many other Muslim nations. The ISI (Inter-Services Intelligence), the secret service of Pakistan, assisted in the training of these 'holy warriors' and also with the logistics of their operations, largely financed by the CIA (Central Intelligence Agency) of the USA. After the ouster of the Soviets when factional infighting emerged among the Afghan people, the ISI trained and equipped the Taliban (literally students), scholars studying Islam in fundamentalist religious institutions on the Afghan-Pakistan border, mainly in the Northwest Frontier and Balochistan provinces. Apparently the Pakistan Frontier Guards regiment had set up camps in the Spin Baldak area of Kandahar to train and equip these Taliban militias before they were sent to fight the Afghan local warlords.[3] It was not only Afghans but also thousands of Pakistanis who were involved in this military enterprise. The other issue was the question of Kashmiri independence from India, and many of the militant outfits operating in Indian-held Kashmir such as the Hizbul Mujahideen were actively assisted by the ISI and other branches of the Pakistan military. Training camps were set up in Pakistan-held Kashmir and other parts of Pakistan for aggression against Indian troops in Kashmir.

---

2 Alawi, Hamza, 'Ethnicity, Muslim Society and the Pakistan Ideology', in Weiss, Anita, M. (ed.) *Islamic Reassertion in Pakistan* (New York, 1986), pp. 21-47, p. 22.

3 Mir, Amir, *The True Face of Jehadis* (Lahore, 2004), p. 21.

The Pakistan government's involvement with Islamic militants later became a liability when after the incidents of 9/11 the United States turned against the Taliban and commenced its war on Islamic militants under the guise of a 'war on terror'. But Pakistan has become an important partner in President Bush's 'war on terrorism'. President Musharaff actively supports the USA in its project and has the unenviable task of reorienting the very same agencies that promoted and supported Islamic militancy to turn against them. As Khaled Ahmed points out, the task of disabusing the fantasy of *Jihad* in Pakistan, where the Muslim masses and the religious leaders in particular are quite alienated from the West and particularly the United States, is a difficult and dangerous venture.[4] Already two attempts have been made on President Musharaff's life and the significant fact is that both were abetted by officers in the Pakistan armed forces. This would indicate a deep disillusionment in the Pakistan military at the *volte-face* of the present leader from its long-standing policies.

In this climate of fostering Islamic militancy and the presence of numerous *Jehadis* and the fundamentalistic measures introduced by Pakistan's most didactic military ruler, Zia ul Haqq, what would be the status of religious minorities, notably Christians? But as mentioned earlier, Pakistan was not envisioned as an Islamic state. Jinnah, in his presidential address in August 1947, the year of independence, to the Constituent Assembly of the new nation had emphasised that, of whatever colour or creed or caste, Pakistanis are first, second and last a citizen of the state with equal privileges, rights and obligations.[5] Jinnah and the other founding fathers of Pakistan had a background, not of Islamic theology and law, but of politics and secular law, not Deoband but Cambridge, Oxford and Lincoln's Inn. They used Islamic idioms and referred to its history but thought in terms of Western political systems. As Afzal Iqbal states, 'There was an incongruity which was visible all around, the spirit soars to the lofty heights reached in Umar's time, but eyes are fastened on the spires of Westminster.'[6] What Jinnah had was a secular vision of Pakistan, a nation founded to ensure the safety and viability of Muslims, but where all religions could subsist on a basis of freedom and equality in law. This was recently pointed out to the Indian public, whose perception is that Jinnah was a communalist who caused the division of India into two states on the basis of religious identity, by L.K. Advani, President of the Hindu-oriented Bharatiya Janatha Party (BJP) of India. This created a furore in India, especially among the BJP ranks and their Hindutva allies, leading ultimately to Advani's resignation from the presidentship of the BJP.

But Advani was entirely correct, however undiplomatic his statement about Jinnah might have been in the Indian context. Jinnah was said to be opposed in principle to mixing religion with politics.[7] The objectives resolution passed by the Constitutional Assembly in March 1949 did reiterate that non-Muslim citizens would not be disadvantaged in any way in Pakistan, but were guaranteed their fundamental rights on a par with Muslim citizens.[8] But Jinnah did not last long. He was a

---

4 Ibid., p. 5.
5 Iqbal, Afzal, *Islamisation of Pakistan* (Delhi, 1984), p. 35.
6 Ibid., p. 24.
7 Ibid., p. 36.
8 Ibid., p. 52.

consumptive and died in 1948, soon after Pakistan became a reality. Even in the first constitution of the nation of 1956 Pakistan was designated as 'The Islamic Republic of Pakistan'. But apparently it was only, as Iqbal states, recognition of intent rather than a *de jure* description of the situation of the country.[9] But even as intent this designation did not augur well for the non-Muslims of Pakistan. Bishop Alexander John Malik, Moderator of the Church of Pakistan, told me in an interview that when this was passed by the Constituent Assembly the religious minority members walked out, but the resolution was nevertheless passed.[10] In the subsequent constitutional revision of 1962 under the aegis of President General Ayyoub Khan also the name Islamic Republic remained in the preamble only. According to Bishop Azariah of Raiwind Diocese, another of my informants, Christians have no problem with this title.[11] The Christians recognise, Bishop Azariah said, that Pakistan is predominantly a Muslim country. What has upset them according to Bishop Azariah is that some of their rights and privileges have been overshadowed by this avowed Islamicity of the nation. I will elaborate on this in subsequent chapters.

It was during the rule of that self-declared champion of Islam, Zia ul Haqq, that Islam was promulgated as the state religion and the Islamicity of the nation moved from its nominal position in the preamble to the main body of the constitution as Art 1 and to a *de jure* significance. Article 227 clarified this still further, stipulating that all existing laws should be brought into conformity with the injunctions of Islam (the personal laws of non-Muslims excepting). This, as can naturally be expected, caused difficulties in a pluralistic democratic state. Though section 14 states that there will be religious freedom, and the personal law of non-Muslims remain intact, these two provisions are evidently contradictory. The affect is that non-Muslims would also be liable to the application of the provisions of the Shari'a. For instance, the prohibition on alcohol meant that Christians have to obtain special permits from the Government to celebrate the Eucharist.

As I.A. Rahim so cogently points out, the effect of laws are not simply confined to those who fall foul of them. It does have an affect on the character of society, its thinking, its attitudes and its prejudices. Rahim says that Pakistan was a more tolerant society before the introduction of the blasphemy law, for instance.[12] Thus the implementation of the Shari'a was bound to have an overall effect on Pakistani society and not just on its Muslim citizens.

The usual norm in an Islamic state is for the Ulama to take a leading role in the governance of the state. The Islamic state is a theocratic state in which the paramount authority is vested in God. The authority of the ruler or rulers is delegated to them by God. Theoretically this means that the people best suited to govern are the ones most knowledgeable about God, Islam and the rules and regulations arising from Islam, namely the Ulama. This is clearly spelt out in the delineation of the Islamic

---

9   Ibid., p. 65.

10 On 5 September 2004.

11 Interviewed on 13 September 2004.

12 Rahim, I.A., 'Questioning the Blasphemy Laws', in Jan, Tarik, *Pakistan between Secularism and Islam: Idolatry, Power and Conflict* (Islamabad, 1998), pp. 241-56, p. 204.

state by both Ayatollah Khomeini and Abul ala Mawdudi.[13] What they envisage is not a parliament of democratically elected politicians but a body of Ulama, selected on the basis of their knowledge of Fiqh, Islamic jurisprudence. But the problem is that the Ulama of Islamic nations are generally looked upon as not in touch with contemporary values and aspirations of the people, especially the youth, and may turn out to be obscurantist and out of touch with the realities of modern life. Iran is a classic example of such a situation as was the former Taliban regime in Afghanistan. The problem with General Zia was that he was not only a fundamentalist himself, but needed the support of the religious elements of the populace for legitimising his undemocratic regime. Perhaps he saw the Islamicisation process as the key to the perpetuation of his dominance in Pakistani affairs. The Jamat I Islami, an organisation known for its fundamentalistic stance, was able to join the Martial Law Administration of Zia, and thus Islamic religious elements were able to participate in governance without ever going through a democratic process. Zia also initiated separate electorates for religious communities. This was undoubtedly detrimental to the formation of a national identity and unity. Bishop Malik calls them 'apartheid electorates'. He emphatically states: 'We are a nation. We should be united. The system of Christians electing Christians and Muslims electing Muslims etc. can be so divisive. So I did not use my vote during Zia's time'.

The Soviet occupation of Afghanistan was a favourable factor for Zia in his Islamicisation quest. The opposition to the Soviet-supported Marxist regime there came from the *mujahideen* (holy warriors). For Zia this was a window of opportunity in which he would be supported by both the West and the Islamic nations. So the Afghan crisis was beneficial to Zia in his Islamicisation of Pakistan and he did not receive the denunciation from the West and non-Islamic nations that normally he could have expected for declaring Pakistan an Islamic state.

It would be fallacious to think that since the vast majority of Pakistanis are Muslim the people there favour a theocratic state. The religious parties are vociferous and united. The Muttahida Majlis Amal, their union, sees to it that they have a visible presence and voice. But as Dr Raziya Sultana, Professor of History in the Qaid I Azam University, Islamabad, stated, 'We are 150 million people and most feel that the duty of the religious people is to look after the mosque rather than deal in political issues. The people feel that the religious people do not have the mind and acumen to handle political issues'. According to Dr Raziya the people in Pakistan are moderate, a fact reiterated by Professor Rasul Baksh, Head of Social Sciences in the prestigious LUMS University, Lahore, and consider religion and politics to be two entirely different things. In their private life they are very religious but in political things they would like to be secular.[14] Malik Iftikhar states, 'Pakistanis desire a closer relationship with the Muslim world and have great concern for the

---

13 See Enayat, Hamid, *Modern Islamic Political Thought* (London, 1982), pp. 101-5.

14 Dr Raziya Sultana, interview 14 September 2004, Professor Baksh, interview 1 September 2004.

welfare of Muslims in other nations, but they are definitely not going to hand over their country to the Mullahs and their regressive type of Islam'.[15]

According to Dr Raziya the NWFP (North West Frontier Province) is the region where Islamic law has been taken seriously and implemented. Professor Baksh corroborated this fact. I have already mentioned that the NWFP is the region where many Taliban had initially been trained as Islamic scholars in Madrasas. The religious parties are in power in this area. This is mainly due to the fact that they are contiguous to Afghanistan where the confrontation of the Taliban with the USA was going on in the Afghan war. The people of the NWFP are of the same ethnic stock, Pushtun, as many of the Afghans who were fighting under the leadership of Mullah Omar. They naturally had sympathies with the plight of their ethnic brethren. The anti-Western and anti-American feeling which is to some extent widespread in Pakistan is felt much more acutely in this region. Thus the religious parties have a stronger hold over the minds of the people and can exploit religious sentiments more readily there. It is to be noted that Musharaff's military action against Islamic militancy and insurgency is mainly concentrated in this region, especially in Waziristan. It is also widely believed that both Mullah Omar and Osama bin Laden are in hiding in this area of Pakistan. The province has a difficult terrain and in British India this was one region over which the British never had full administrative control. The Pushtun are traditionally a war-like people anyway and difficult to govern. But Dr Raziya is sceptical about the success of religious parties even there in normal times. Dr Raziya herself hails from this region and should be familiar with the popular mood there.

General Zia also promulgated Hudood laws as part of the law of the country. Hudood laws (from the Arabic *Hudd*, pl. *Hudud*, meaning limits) are laws pertaining to criminal jurisprudence.[16] This includes draconian penalties such as stoning to death for *zina* (fornication) and amputation of arms for theft. These laws are especially detrimental to minority groups and women. The law of evidence, which was also altered to bring it into consonance with the implementation of Islamic law, meant that the evidence of male Muslims took precedence over others. Hassan Abbas points out that the nature of the evidence was such that the complaint of rape by a woman, for instance, becomes a confession to be compounded by medical examination or a pregnancy so that the accuser eventually became the accused and was charged with fornication.[17] It is said that 80 per cent of women charged under the hudood laws are innocent.[18] Punishments under hudood laws are also awarded by the British model secular courts but appeal can be sought at the Federal Shari'a court.

The law that has caused the greatest disquiet in Christian minds is the Blasphemy Law. This law is liable to much abuse to settle personal scores against enemies and especially Christians, since Christians are anyway suspected of an attitude of contempt

---

15 Malik, Iftikhar, *Islam, Nationalism and the West: Issues of Identity in Pakistan* (London, 1999), p. 137.

16 The ideal in Islam is perfect freedom. But limits (*hudood*) have to be prescribed to freedom to enable an orderly society, so that unmitigated and uncurbed freedom of the individual will not push society into chaos.

17 Abbas, Hassan, *Pakistan's Drift into Extremism* (New York, 2005), p. 103.

18 *The Christian Voice* (29 August 2004): 4.

for Islamic beliefs and practices. The law covers much ground, such as damaging and defiling places of worship, disturbing religious assemblies, trespassing on burial grounds, and uttering disparaging words in order to wound religious feelings. All these are grounds for the application of this law. The law was initially instituted in 1860 by the British in order to obviate religious riots between faith communities, but General Zia expanded the provisions and made the penalties more rigorous. For instance, in addition to the section (295) on defiling the Holy Qur'an, disparaging the person of Prophet Muhammad (equal to high treason), derogatory remarks about the *Ummul Mumineen* (Muslim community), the *Ahl al Bait* (The Prophet's family), *Khulafer Rashidun* (The Rightly Guided Caliphs) and the *Sahaba* (Companions of the Prophet) were added in section 298A.[19] The alternative penalty of life imprisonment for defaming the Prophet was challenged in the Federal Shari'a court in 1990 and quashed by the panel of Muslim judges there resulting in a mandatory death sentence on conviction. The court was of the opinion that the alternative penalty provision was un-Islamic and conflicted with the constitutional provision that all laws should be brought into conformity with the Shari'a.[20]

Often the allegation of blasphemy and the prosecution are initiated not by the police but by private individuals. Even if the accused are acquitted they may face execution by vigilantes such as the Sipah-I-Sahaba (Soldiers of the Prophet's Companions) or such militant groups. In one case a Christian, Samuel Masih, accused of blasphemy was attacked and killed by a Muslim policeman guarding him in prison.[21] Even if they were not killed it would be difficult for the accused to overcome the stigma and damaged reputation that he/she has suffered. Often their only option would be to leave Pakistan.[22] Fear of social ostracisation by Muslims, the stigma attached to accusations of blasphemy and fear of reprisals by extremists would make life unbearable for the accused in Pakistan in spite of the fact that a court had exonerated him/her. Most of these cases are against Christians, and lawyers are even apprehensive of defending the accused for fear of reprisals by Islamic militants.[23] There are several cases pending. Some of these allegations are brought to favour a business transaction or to settle personal scores. For instance a Christian may refuse to sell or move from land needed by a Muslim and the latter may fabricate an allegation of blasphemy against the recalcitrant Christian. The motivation of accusation of blasphemy might well also be a prior grudge against a Christian. Linda Walbridge opines that many of these accusations of blasphemy are brought frivolously and arbitrarily but result in the loss by the accused of jobs, homes and contact with their family and friends.[24]

The Blasphemy Law has also implications for intellectual liberty and freedom of speech. A similar problem now exists in Western nations with the introduction of laws

---

19 Ghazi, Mahmud A., 'The law of Tahiri-I-Risalat: A social, political and historical perspective', pp. 209-40, in Tarik Jan, p. 217.
20 Ghazi, MA, p. 220.
21 *The Christian Voice* (6 June 2004).
22 As mentioned in *The Christian Voice* (20 June 2004): 5.
23 Malik, Iftikhar, p. 303.
24 Walbridge, Linda, *The Christians of Pakistan* (London, 2003), p. ix.

against inciting religious hatred. This is basically the reason the British introduced a blasphemy law in India, namely prevention of inter-religious conflict. But an honest and rational criticism of a religion is a legitimate human activity. The analytical study of religion might give rise to occasions of criticism of certain aspects of a religion, be it the ritual, doctrinal or even theological aspects. In many a case such legitimate criticism could be misinterpreted as blasphemy or inciting religious hatred. The law in Pakistan as it stands is vague and ill-defined and liable to misinterpretation and misuse. As indeed the comedian Rowan Atkinson pointed out regarding the new law in Britain, there might even be instances when a joke or a caricature of a religion, which is intended to entertain rather than wound religious sensibilities, might be construed as inciting religious hatred. I.A. Rahim points out that often blasphemy is equated with heresy, that is honest dissent with a religious belief, practice or opinion. He goes on further to suggest that the potential of blasphemy may not be confined to purely religious matters such as theology but might cover dissent in politics, economy and social thinking.[25]

Though no one has as yet been executed for the offence of blasphemy, some have been convicted and are going through an appeal process. A notable case is that of Ayyoub Masih, whose conviction was on the basis of having praised Salman Rushdie's Satanic Verses. The law of blasphemy in Pakistan became a *cause celebre* when Bishop John Joseph, the first Roman Catholic Pakistani Bishop, shot himself to death in front of the sessions court of Sahiwal near Lahore in May 1998 as protest against Ayyoub's conviction. The Bishop's suicide brought the Blasphemy Law into the limelight and gave it international publicity.

Zia most probably brought this law into implementation as appeasement of the religious parties with the intention of securing their cooperation and support for his illegitimate regime. But its effect has been to foster a climate of hostility, intolerance and apprehension on the part of religious minorities. They and human rights groups are vehemently opposed to the blasphemy and Hudood Laws and would like them to be repealed.[26] However there has been no move to repeal them. Professor Baksh is of the opinion that General Musharaff is waiting for the right political circumstances and climate of opinion to make a move to repeal the laws. There is no doubt that the religious parties will hotly oppose such a move. The recent agreements reached by President Musharaff with the MMA makes it look unlikely in the near future. President Musharaff needs their support in the present political climate in Pakistan. Indeed the *Friday Times* reports that the MMA will vehemently oppose any amendments to the Blasphemy Law.[27] Even Benazir Bhutto's secular PPP is divided over the issue of the Blasphemy Law. As recently as 2004 the Minister for Religion, Ijazul Haqq, is reported to have warned that the people of Pakistan would come out on the streets if there were any attempt to change the Blasphemy Law.[28] On another occasion he is reported to have stated that the law of the jungle will prevail if these statutes are

---

25 Rahim, I.A., p. 202.
26 *The Christian Voice*, 29 August 2004, p. 4.
27 *Friday Times* (3-9 September 2004): 15.
28 Ibid.

ever abrogated.[29] The minister is no doubt being unduly pessimistic, but this is only a reflection of the apprehension of Musharaff's government over the feelings of the masses on the issue of the Blasphemy Law and Hudood laws. As Dr Raziya pointed out to me, the people in the West think that Musharaff's is a military regime and very strong.[30] This is a fallacy, she said. It is in reality a military-civil combination, meaning that the military administration of Pakistan cannot ignore civil sensibilities and need their cooperation. She pointed out that the religious parties have made it into the provincial assemblies and into the National Assembly also. So they are a power to reckon with, especially in these times when they can portray Islam as a victim of Western hegemony. There is popular sympathy with Islamic resurgence and opposition to the USA. So the religious parties are now a power to negotiate with. Musharaff's Government is not a stable one and things in Pakistan are fluid. President Musharaff is seen by the minorities as fair and just and sympathetic to their misgivings[31] and wish to counter the impact of hard-line laws, but political bargaining is always going on, and he has to tread cautiously.

President Musharaff has however instituted some safeguards to prevent the abuse of the Blasphemy Law. False accusations of blasphemy can attract the penalty of ten years' imprisonment for the accuser. The Chief district authority or a magistrate is supposed to investigate a blasphemy allegation to test its *bona fides* before the case is registered.[32] This provision has met with stiff resistance from the religious parties. Punjab and Balochistan Assemblies have passed resolutions against this amendment to the Blasphemy Law. However, the Central Government has passed these amendments. But in practice these safeguards do not operate satisfactorily. The Deputy District Commissioner and the Magistrate may not have the time or the inclination to investigate allegations sufficiently thoroughly and may take the easiest option of registering cases straightaway. Often the victims are from poor and uneducated backgrounds and may possess little acumen to protest or argue against allegations. I have already mentioned that they may not get legal help, as lawyers are reluctant to take up such cases.

The origins of Christianity in Pakistan are not very clear. There is a belief, at any rate among the Christians of Pakistan, that the church there had its origins as early as the First Century CE, and was established by St Thomas the Apostle. In my next chapter I will discuss the issue in detail, but Bishop John Malik categorically stated that the apostle had come to Taxila (Takshashila), the famous university city of ancient India. He came by the River Sin, which passes to the north of Taxila, after landing at Karachi by sea. The Marthoma Church believes he came to Kerala, India, in 52 CE and they adduce proofs for his presence in Kerala. Bishop Malik stated that St Thomas went to Kerala after establishing a church in Pakistan. The Taxila Cross which the Church of Pakistan has adopted as its icon is a vestige apparently of this ancient church in the vicinities of Taxila established by Apostle Thomas. During

---

29 *The Times* (11 May 1998).
30 Dr Raziya Sultana, interview 14 September 2004.
31 Mrs Imtiaz, in interview 12 September 2004.
32 Ghazzali, Abdul Sattar, *Islamic Pakistan: Illusions, and Reality* (Islamabad, 1996), p. 237.

Akbar's reign a church had existed in Lahore used by Armenian Christian traders. Akbar was sympathetic to other faiths, and in his court Syrian and Roman Catholic priests had spent time in theological discussion with Akbar and Muslim and Hindu scholars, an early forerunner of inter-religious dialogue.

The real growth of Christianity however came in the 19th Century and was the result of the efforts of the missionary movement of that era in Europe and the USA. It comprised all denominations. The missionary zeal and fervour in Europe and America at that time resulted in the British Government relaxing its step-motherly attitude to Christian missions (the British were loath to interfere in the religious matters of their subjects, no doubt fearing a backlash from the natives) and through the Charter Act of 1813 permitted missionary activity in British India. The CMS (Church Missionary Society) and the USPG (United Society for the Propagation of the Gospel) were evangelistic wings of the Official church of India of the time, the Anglican Church of India, Burma (Myanmar) and Ceylon (Sri Lanka). The initial successes of Christianity were mainly in the Punjab province and many of them migrated to other provinces in due course. There were very few in Sind and Balochistan in the early stages and the ones in the Sind were mainly migrants from Goa. Bishop Malik informed me that now Christians are to be seen in all provinces, including the NWFP.

One interesting phenomenon is all-Christian villages. These were started by missionaries in the vicinity of canals which provided water for irrigation, and thus facilitated the establishment of farming colonies. According to Bishop Malik there are at least, if not more than, two dozen Christian villages. The names of some villages also reveal their Christian character. Martinpur, for instance, would apparently be named after a Western missionary. Since the land holdings have become rather small and unable to provide a livelihood for the owners many of the Christians have moved out, and settled into other areas. This dispersion would certainly offer them less security than if they were congregated into particular Christian village enclaves.

The Christian community of Pakistan is basically a struggling community. Due to their origins in socially discriminated Hindu castes, the so-called 'untouchables', they are where they are now only due to the dedication and efforts of their parents. Unlike many other Christian communities of the subcontinent, the Christians of Kerala for instance, they did not come from an affluent social background. They are mainly converts from among the Chuhras, a caste engaged in sweeping streets and such 'polluting' occupations, and to some extent the affects of the stigma of their antecedents are still with them. Bishop Azariah said that there might be some Christians such as the Anglo-Indians, some members of the armed forces in British times, and some bureaucrats who belonged to a higher social class. But the general Christian community is a Punjabi-based Christian community whose fathers and forefathers have struggled to bring their descendents to where they are now. Bishop Azariah is of the opinion that they cannot have much of a say in government policy unless the Christians build up a base in Parliament, politics, and intellectual activities such as research or science. They are striving hard to survive and live a decent life. Converts from such a low economic and social background had to overcome the resentment of Muslims, who thought this mass conversion of untouchables to Christianity would disrupt society, and even reservations among the

Western missionaries, who feared that they would antagonise prospective Christian converts from higher castes by admitting Chuhras into the Christian faith. Chuhras were subject to rampant discrimination, and they were also considered dirty, undisciplined, prone to drunkenness, bad manners, lack of ambition and dependency on others.[33] They had to battle all these resentments and disparagement even after becoming Christian.

The Christians did not migrate to India during partition as their Hindu compatriots did. There has been debate about the status of Christians in Pakistan, which I will detail in Chapter 5. Are they *dhimmi* (protected citizens) as some Muslim fundamentalists argue, or are they full-fledged citizens of Pakistan? But the Christians are not in Pakistan by virtue of conquest, as *dhimm*i are required to be. They are here by an accident of history after being citizens of British India for a very long time. The question of Christians being *dhimmi* and jizya (a special tax levied from *dhimmi*) have been raised even in the Ministry of Religious affairs.[34] In an Islamic state the *dhimmi* cannot be members of the Shura (Consultative Council). However, the Christians feel that they are as much Pakistani as the Muslim citizens. Bishop Malik points out that the Christians have played as much a part in the creation of Pakistan as anyone else. He states that the religious minorities of India and Pakistan have also fought for independence from colonial rule. Joshua Fazl-ud-din points out that after Independence the Christians cast off the mantle of neutrality and whole-heartedly allied themselves with the state in which they found themselves.[35] This implies that before partition they might not have taken an active part in the independence movement but might have remained neutral in the tussle between the British and the Muslim and Hindu nationalists.[36] This is debatable as there are many instances of Indian Christians having acted fervently to win freedom from colonial rule. Joshua mentions that Christians have adjusted well to partition.[37] They certainly stayed where they were, though Christian tenants of Hindu Zamindaris faced problems when the land ownership was taken over by Muslims.

Bishop Azariah remarked that Muslims should relate well to the Christians since the Qur'an has a definite place for Christianity, and this is a faith that should be respected by Muslims. Indeed the Christians are to Muslims *ahl al Kitab* (People who share scriptures with the Muslims). The Qur'an actually states:

Strongest among men in enmity
To the believers wilt thou
Find the Jews and pagans;
And nearest among them in love wilt thou
Find those who say
'We are the Christians' (Sura 5:85)

---

33 Walbridge, pp. 16-17.
34 Butler and Chagathai, p. 344.
35 Fazl-ud-din, Joshua, *The Future of Christians in Pakistan* (Lahore, 1949), p. 39
36 Ibid.
37 Ibid., p. 40.

So the Qur'an has explicitly confirmed this special relationship between Muslims and Christians *vis à vis* other faiths.

Part of the problem in Muslim-Christian relations is that the Muslim community sometimes tends to identify the Christians with the former colonial regime or with the West and this would induce some hostility to them. This perspective is entirely fallacious and culturally the Christians of Pakistan are quite indigenous, be it the matter of their dress, their language, their home decor or culinary habits. However, in the churches the style of worship, the use of Western music, and church architecture and decor inherited from the British can sometimes generate this view of Christians. Indeed, Joshua Fazl-ud-din, writing in 1949, advises Pakistani Christians to indigenise.[38] The Christian leaders have taken indigenisation of the church and worship seriously. Bishop Malik said that they are keen to indigenise. He admitted that the Christian liturgy in Pakistan is too Western in its orientation, and they need to change this and introduce cultural changes in worship, for instance use Church music in the Pakistani idiom. Not all Christians approve of such changes, especially those of the older generation, since change is uncomfortable, as the Bishop said. I noticed that most Christians use Arabic names, names which are popular with Muslims. Bishop Malik pointed out that these are names common to Christians and Muslims, since many of the names are to be found in the Christian scriptures as well. This again reiterates the affinity between the two religions.

The low status of the origins of the Christian community as from untouchable groups such as the Chuhras would also induce the Muslim community to look down on them. They are still a struggling community in economic, political and social senses. It is easy for the majority community to stigmatise and patronise such a community, leading to discrimination and ignorance of their plight. The identification of the state as Islamic would also make them uncomfortable and subject to pressure. It is to be noted that some of them have been tried under Shari'a laws and have been subjected to the consequences.[39] A number of them have been victimised by the Blasphemy Law. It is difficult for Christians to get out of their religious skin and conform to the Islamic nature of the Pakistani civil society.

Moreover, in a pluralistic democracy there is no need to do this. A Pakistani Christian studying in England once told me that Pakistani Christians find it difficult to be loyal to the state as it is constituted now. This is no doubt due to the feeling that they are a kind of second class citizens,[40] which is exactly what the religious parities are demanding for non-Muslims in Pakistan, i.e. a *dhimmi* status. Some Christians have succumbed to pressure and become Muslims. Some have done so to avail of the easier divorce laws in Islam, particularly for males. Divorce is only possible for Christians on grounds of adultery. It is difficult to prove adultery and moreover such accusations will invite the application of the draconian penalties for fornication under the Hudood Laws. Moreover, since Muslims are not allowed to marry non-Muslims, a Christian/Hindu marriage will stand dissolved if one of the partners converted to

---

38 Fazl-ud-din, p. 45.
39 Bishop Azariah, in interview 13 September 2004.
40 Butler, R.A. and Chagathai, M.I., *Trying to Respond* (Lahore, 1994), p. 345.

Islam.[41] Conversely, in some cases Christian girls have been abducted by Muslims and a Mullah will declare her (on being bribed by the abductor) to have converted to Islam.[42] This will at once prohibit her from returning to her Christian parents since that would amount to apostasy, an action that invites heavy penalties under Islamic Law, even death. The higher status and privileges of Muslims in Pakistan will also be an inducement for some Christians to convert to Islam.

Christians also face problems in the sphere of education. Christian schools are free of Governmental interference and have a reputation for higher standards and therefore are popular with Muslims also. Many of the national leaders of Pakistan were educated in Christian schools. However there are problems with the curriculum and with textbooks. Christian students can study Christian Religious Education up to grade eight. But from grade nine they have to opt for either the study of Islam or Civics. However, the choosing of Civics mark them out as hostile to Islam, and since most of the teaching staff are Muslims the students may be discriminated against in marking. Bishop Malik said that he encourages his flock to study Islam. This is so that they can get better marks and also learn about Islam, thereby improving inter-religious relations in the country.

Another question is the misrepresentation of Christianity in textbooks. In some cases the textbooks seem to say that all Pakistanis are Muslims. In another context Christianity is described as polytheistic. This perspective has infiltrated not only religion-related subjects but also secular subjects such as History or Geography. Bishop Azariah mentioned some examples of pejorative writing. 'Who lives in Pakistan? – Muslims'. 'Pakistan belongs to the Muslims of Pakistan'. These statements in textbooks do not take into account the presence of religious minorities of Pakistan who truly believe they are also sons of the soil. Such fallacious statements in textbooks have the dangerous effect of alienating religious minorities from society at an early age. Also the Bishop stated that in History Christian-Muslim relations are depicted very negatively. The only matters mentioned are the Crusades and the colonial era. The bad descriptions of Christianity found in textbooks are written by Muslims. Christians are demanding that discussions of Christianity in textbooks should either be written by Christian authors or eliminated altogether.[43]

In spite of all these adverse circumstances there have been attempts to improve inter-religious relations. The Ministry of Religious and Minority Affairs is a body that has been instituted to safeguard the constitutional rights and welfare of minorities. The Federal Advisory Council for Minority Affairs is another organisation with minority representatives. District Minority Committees also exist. In 1985 a non-lapsable special fund for the uplift and welfare of minorities has also been created. One of its remits is to assist financially individuals and families in dire straits. Acquisition of land for cemeteries is another. The National Commission for Minorities established in 1993 is another body constituted for safeguarding the interests of minorities. Bishop Azariah sounds a note of caution: 'The Ministry of Minority affairs is there,

---

41 Justice and Peace Commission Report (18 July 2004), p. 4.
42 Bishop John Malik, in interview 5 September 2004.
43 Ibid.

and they listen to the concerns of the minorities. How effective they are has to be seen and evaluated as time goes along'.[44]

The sporadic violent incidents against churches and Christians, the Blasphemy Law and even the Islamicisation of Pakistan have filled the Christians with a sense of foreboding and despondency. This is even more so in the case of such a socially and economically struggling community as the Christians. They tend to see Islam as a steamroller force and to panic. This might give rise to a ghetto mentality. Justice Cornelius writing in *The Christian Voice* in 1953 warns against 'A general feeling of despair, a widespread lack of confidence and a common readiness to anticipate the worst'.[45]

But do the Christians of Pakistan have cause to hope? There is much endeavour to promote Christian–Muslim dialogue. The initiative for this is mainly from the Christians, though many Muslims do participate and might desire good relations between the two communities. Bishop Malik stated that the initiative is from the Christian side because they are in a minority situation and consequently more vulnerable, and they desire dialogue for reasons of peaceful coexistence and removal of mutual misunderstanding.[46]

The Christian Study Centre in Rawalpindi set up in 1968 is one of the instances of Christian Initiative for promoting understanding between Christians and Muslims. I saw many Muslim researchers use it as a resource for their studies. The Centre is residential and Muslim and Christian scholars live there side by side. Its journal *al Mushir* has articles in both Urdu and English. Themes on Christian-Muslim dialogue are emphasised. The Centre engages in teaching Islamics to Christians and *vice versa* if required to do so. The Centre has established contacts with Muslim scholars in the Islamic Research Institute, Islamabad. Papers and articles on each other are exchanged for appraisal and constructive criticism by the two bodies before being published so as to avoid any distortion or misrepresentation of Islam and Christianity. Loyola Hall in Lahore is another such institution for promoting inter-religious dialogue. Regular meetings of a Muslim-Christian discussion group are held under the auspices of the Hall.

According to Butler and Chagathai Christian-Muslim relations are best in cosmopolitan Karachi.[47] This implies that relations are not so harmonious in other urban centres and rural areas. This might be because caste prejudices still abound in the countryside and in cities where Christians originate from low caste groups, and might induce Muslims to look down upon Christians. It might be pointed out that many of the Christians in Karachi are of Goan and Anglo-Indian antecedents and hail from a better social and economic class. But again they might be categorised as Westerners, not Pakistani.

In the following chapters I will discuss in detail some of the issues outlined in this chapter. Christian-Muslim relations in Pakistan involve some complex issues and a diverse range of factors. I have made use of both published resources as

---

44 Bishop Azariah, Interview 13 September 2004.
45 Butler R.A. and Chagathai, M.I., p. 336.
46 Bishop Malik, Interview 5 September 2004.
47 Butler and Chagathai, p. 328.

well as interviews with Christians and Muslims, academics, journalists, politicians and ordinary citizens to clarify these issues. I hope the discussions will bring out a balanced perspective of inter-faith relations, and the role that Islam plays in Pakistan. Being an important religious minority, good relations between Christians and Muslims are important for Pakistan, and will establish it as a modern state where human rights in general and the rights of minorities in particular are safeguarded, both under the law as well as by good inter-personal relationships between the two faith communities.

Chapter Two

The origins of Christianity in Pakistan

In this short chapter I am not setting out to give a systematic account of the history of Christianity in Pakistan but only trying to provide an essential background to enlighten the study of Christian-Muslim relations there.

I have already mentioned in Chapter 1 that the Christians in Pakistan believe that Christianity came to them at the very outset of the religion, i.e. in the first century CE, through St Thomas, the apostle who is well known in the Gospels as 'doubting Thomas'. There is a strong tradition among the Christians of Kerala in South India also that St Thomas came and established the ancient church there now called the Mar Thoma or the Syrian Orthodox Church. The place where St Thomas was martyred by a Tamil king is to be found on St Thomas Mount, a suburb of Chennai (Madras). The Kerala Christians state that St Thomas came only to South India. However, Pakistani Christians believe that St Thomas came initially from the Holy Land to Pakistan before going to Kerala. Apparently he came to Taxila (Takshashila) by means of the river Sin 20 kilometres north of Taxila that goes all the way to the port town of Karachi. Bishop Malik of the Church of Pakistan believes he came to the Taxila region by this river.[1] Taxila is well known as an ancient seat of Hindu and Buddhist learning. The Taxila Cross, now the icon of the Church of Pakistan, is said to be a vestige of St Thomas's presence in Taxila. Apparently St Thomas was enslaved and taken to the Indian subcontinent by an Indian called Habban.[2] Habban presented St Thomas to the legendary king Gondophares at Taxila, who ruled an Indo-Parthian kingdom from 21 AD for at least 26 years.[3] These details are to be found in the apocryphal *Acts of St Thomas*, a document whose credibility has been doubted by scholars.[4] The discovery in 1854 by General Alexander Cunningham of coins bearing the image of Gondophares in Afghanistan brought Gondophares from legend to historical reality. The cruciform bases of stupas (pillars) in Taxila are taken as further evidence of the presence of St Thomas there. The Taxila Cross as I mentioned above has been adopted by the Church of Pakistan as its icon from 1970.

An interesting belief among some Christian scholars is that the Holy Shroud of Turin was originally woven in Sind. Herodotus the fifth century historian uses the word Sindon for the Shroud.[5]

---

1   In interview 5 September 2004.
2   Young, William G., *Days of Small Things* (Rawalpindi, 1991), p. 30.
3   Wikipedia Encyclopaedia, http://en.wikipedia.org/wiki/Gondophares.
4   Ibid.
5   Rooney, John, *Shadows in the Dark* (Rawalpindi, 1984), p. 27.

Further evidence of St Thomas's advent to Taxila is a village nearby called Karm Thoma, where apparently St Thomas saved the people from a natural disaster. Moreover, the Sufi group known as Thatta Nagar Fakirs, though seen to be affiliated to Islam, practise Christian rites and possess a book claimed to be the Gospel of St Matthew.[6] The Thatta Nagar Fakirs call themselves Barthamai (Sons of Thomas), i.e. descendants of the church established by St Thomas. Another interesting belief is that Melchior, one of the magi who visited the infant Jesus in Bethlehem, was a scholar from the University of Taxila.[7]

By the fifth century CE the Churches in the north Indian subcontinent had come under the control of the Church of Persia, under the Catholicos, the Patriarch of Seleucia. Churches in the Sind, South India and Mumbai (Bombay) came under the Metropolitan See of Riv-Ardeshir. However, from the tenth to the sixteenth century CE Christianity seems to have declined and almost disappeared in Northern India probably due to the Buddhist movements that came with the Kushan Kings who defeated Gondophares in AD 60 and established their suzerainty in the Pakistan region. Muhammad Ibn Quasim, the first Muslim invader of the region in 711-712 CE found the native population to be mainly Buddhist. Rooney states that the decline in the Persian church consequent to the conquest of Persia by Muslims must have also contributed to the disappearance of Christianity from Pakistan.[8]

The next episode in the history of Christianity in Pakistan comes with the efforts of Jesuit missionaries to convert Akbar, the Mughal emperor, on the premise that the conversion of such a great emperor will result in the conversion of the masses in his empire. Now Akbar himself had formulated a new religion, Din Ilahi (Religion of God), that is presumed to be a synthesis of the religions he was familiar with such as Islam, Christianity and Hinduism. Din Ilahi, though Akbar gained converts in his court, failed to make much of an impact on the masses. Thus it was not valid to believe that the conversion of Akbar to Christianity would be influential on his subjects. Therefore, the intent of the first and second Jesuit missions apparently failed. The third Jesuit mission more wisely decided on focusing on local conversions and at the same time keeping the Mughal emperor happy, an important prerequisite to the smooth functioning of the evangelists.

The Mughal emperors, except for Aurangazeb, were tolerant and ecumenically minded and thus did not pose any problems for Christian evangelisation in Northern India. Jehangir, Akbar's successor, for instance, is said to have worn a golden crucifix on his neck and made generous gifts to the churches in Lahore and Agra.[9] Rooney attributes the failure of the Jesuit missions to Jehangir employing the Jesuit missionaries as his envoys on diplomatic assignments, which may have lessened their spiritual impact.[10] Muslim jealousy of Christian influence in court may have been an added factor. Anyway, from the mid-eighteenth to the nineteenth century there is no trace of Christianity in the history of the Pakistan region.

---

6   Young, p. 45.
7   Young, p. 72.
8   Ibid., p. 106.
9   Rooney, John, *The Hesitant Dawn* (Rawalpindi, 1984), p. 58.
10 Ibid., p. 97.

The arrival of British armies and the railway to the Punjab and Sind was the catalyst for Christian presence in the Pakistan region in the nineteenth century. The churches received grant in aid from the British government for teaching in and running the Railway schools, and with this income established their own schools and orphanages. Though the churches' activities were thus necessarily restricted to the cantonments, they set up an infrastructure that would help later to sustain and support the conversions that came in the latter half of the nineteenth century and early twentieth century.

Many South Indian Christians and Goans accompanied the army. This was pragmatic since the British officers consumed beef, pork and alcoholic beverages and the Hindus and Muslims would not touch these substances. Therefore, the only option was to employ Christians. The presence of Goans was particularly interesting at that time. They were Portuguese nationals and hence to be eligible for employment in the British Army they had to identify themselves as Anglo-Indians. This apparently was done by anglicising their Portuguese surnames.[11] Even now in Pakistan the Goans are looked upon more as Westerners than as Pakistanis.

Similarly, to further their objectives the railway companies invited investment from Missionary societies, promising that the railways would be an asset in carrying the Gospel to the farthest corners of the empire.

The British East India Company was not too interested in spreading Christianity in India. Their primary objective was making profit from trade and they perhaps felt that they should not antagonise the local people by proselytising them. Linda Walbridge says that they sought good rapport with the native population by contributing to Muslim processions and maintenance of temples and supervising pilgrimages to sacred sites in India.[12] But in 1813 the British Parliament voted to persuade the Company to allow Christian missionaries to India. By 1850 apparently the British Government of India also decided to protect the properties and interests of Christian converts, thereby making evangelisation of Hindus and Muslims easier.

It was in the latter half of the nineteenth century that Christian evangelisation gathered pace. Three names prominent in the Protestant Missions (United Presbyterian Mission) are that of Harper, Youngson and Bailey. They are said to have progressed the groundwork for the next decade. 1874-1885 is termed the age of Harper. Harper was a graduate of Aberdeen who decried offering worldly incentives for conversion. Harper was also reluctant to convert members of low social status. Perhaps he was of the view that conversions from the upper castes would be more productive in attracting Hindus to the Christian fraternity. A similar approach could be seen in the well-known Catholic missionary De Nobili (1577-1656) from Italy, who evangelised in the Tamilnadu and Karnataka regions of India. In his zeal to convert Brahmins, De Nobili adopted their life style and dress and sported the kuduma (tuft of hair on shaven head) and cut himself off completely from other missionaries.

Sialkot city was the exclusive centre of operations of the United Presbyterian Mission. Schools were a useful instrument for propagating Christianity. Knowledge of English was becoming an important prerequisite to successful careers, especially

11 Rooney, John, *Symphony on Sands* (Rawalpindi, 1988), p. 22.
12 Walbridge, Linda, *The Christians of Pakistan* (London, 2003), p. 7.

in state departments in British India, and therefore people who entered Christian mission schools had an edge over their compatriots since the standard of teaching English in Christian schools was better and still is. Bishop Malik told me that many of the leaders of Pakistan graduated from Christian schools. These schools had an agenda of transforming the people and Westernising them as *preparatio evangelica*, for in their eyes Western civilisation and Christianity were synonymous. They held the erroneous belief that Hindu civilisation would crumble in the face of Western education and civilisation, a premise that has now been proved wrong. They trusted in, as Dharmaraja states, 'The transcendent power of Western education and universality of English literature'.[13] Religious Education in schools was considered by the missionaries as the best mode of evangelisation. Initially the schools were targeting high caste Hindus and high class Muslims, thinking that their conversion would lead all Pakistanis and Indians to Christ. It was only after the departure of Harper, who was reluctant to convert people of low social status, that Youngson began a mass conversion movement of untouchables and such people of low social standing.[14] The fear was that conversion of low caste people would put off others from joining the Christian fold, since the caste system and its prejudices were so deeply ingrained in the Pakistani psyche. For instance, members of a weaver caste had stopped converting when the Chuhras became Christian in substantial numbers.[15] It is to be noted that the Chuhras engaged in cleaning streets and toilets were at the bottom of the caste ladder.

The American missionaries, especially the United Presbyterian Mission, was *avante garde* in the sense that they decided to aim their evangelisation at not only the higher echelons of society but at all. Sialkot city was the exclusive sphere of operations of the United Presbyterian Mission. This led to conversion to Christianity being a sort of mass movement in the Panjab. Mass conversions were not entirely to the liking of the missionaries since to them the acceptance of Christ was essentially a personal and individual matter and not driven by caste, politics or other extraneous factors. But to many Chuhras and such outcastes or untouchables conversion was one of the avenues for escaping the oppressive caste system. They viewed Christianity as a socially liberating force.

The saga of conversion reveals that the Church carefully considered social and economic conditions of the people whose evangelisation was sought before embarking on evangelisation. In some cases evangelisation was abandoned. Matters such as caste hierarchies and language (the linguistic groups of Kutchi and Parkari Kohlis are instances) were taken into account. In some cases the Roman Catholic Church decided that evangelisation of certain ethnic groups was best left to the Protestant missions. Work on Marwari Bhils was abandoned by the Roman church in favour of Protestant missions.[16] This mitigates to some extent the common charge that Christian

---

13 Dharmaraja, Jacob, *Colonialism and Christian Mission: Post-Colonial Reflections* (New Delhi, 1993), p. 58.

14 Young, p. 8.

15 See Walbridge, op. cit., p. 16.

16 Rooney, *Symphony on Sands*, p. 92.

missionary enterprise was a sledge hammer that did not taken into cognizance the cultural and economic characteristics of their evangelistic constituencies.

The first Muslim convert to Christianity was one Sayyid Daud Shah, the result of bazaar preaching by catechists of the UP Mission. A Christian bookshop was opened in Sialkot in 1877. Even a moulavi (Alim), Akbar Ali, was converted by Youngson.

But the majority of conversions to Christianity came from the Chuhar community, an untouchable community whose main occupation was sweeping streets, a polluting occupation in the Hindu caste hierarchy. The motivation here could have been spiritual but it was also that they saw Christianity as an avenue for escaping caste-based discrimination. Apparently a number of them were also attracted by Sufism for the same reasons.[17] These converts were known as Naseri and Isai (from the Arabic terms for Nazarene and Jesus).

In Lahore, conversions became a mass movement in 1889 and continued for several decades into the 1930s. In September 1889 alone 75 Punjabis were converted by Protestant Missions. The Balmiki is another group that turned to Christianity to escape persecution. The Balmikis consider themselves to be both Hindus and Sikhs but they chose to stay in Pakistan during partition. Probably they suffered for this decision, and many chose to convert to Christianity and change their religious identity. The Mazhabi is another low caste Sikh community that turned to Christianity to escape discrimination. In the colonial days to some extent Christianity was identified with the ruling power, the British, and to become a Christian was thought to confer some of the reflected glory of the rulers on the converts.

Migration of Christians

On national independence many Christians had to leave the Panjab to make way for Muslim refugees from India. They had to give up their lands for the incoming Muslims. This was evidently unfair, but in the unsettled climate of those days and the perception that Pakistan was to be a homeland for Muslims, the rights of the evicted Christians were ignored. Secondly, Muslim refugees replaced many of the Hindu landlords who had fled to India, and the Christians found their new masters less compatible and certainly having less experience of managing the farms. The outcome was the movement of many Panjabi Christians to Karachi. Thus the composition of the Christian population of Karachi changed drastically. Formerly they were predominantly Goan. But now almost 95 per cent of Christians are of Panjabi ethnicity.[18] Moreover, many Goans wanted to migrate to the West. When immigration to the United Kingdom became progressively more difficult they opted to move to Australia. Apparently the church did not encourage such migration, since they felt that this would be construed by Pakistan as Christian disloyalty to and mistrust of Pakistan. This brings to mind the statement of Roman Catholic Bishop Andrew Francis of Multan that the Christians of Pakistan do not look to Western nations but to the President and Prime Minister of Pakistan for leadership.[19] However,

---

17 Singh, Yoginder, in 'Where the Twain shall Meet', *The South Asian.Com*, May 2005.
18 Rooney, *Symphony on Sands*, p. 103.
19 Reported in *The Christian Voice* (1 February 2004).

more than half of the Goans are said to have left Pakistan permanently. Openings for lucrative employment in the Persian Gulf was another factor, this time among Panjabi Christians. This has led to disruptions in family life, though economic status increased, the lack of parental control over children being an adverse circumstance.

Movement between churches by Panjabi Christians is also notable. The Protestant denominations gained by such movement. Rooney opines that the migrants from the Punjab found more real fellowship in the local independent churches than in the Catholic churches.[20] Another factor that is alleged is that the latter enticed Catholics away by promise of employment. It is to be noted that the displaced persons were in hardship and had originally to be content with menial jobs.

Many Catholic Bengalis are said to have migrated to Bangladesh consequent on the declaration of independence of East Pakistan and secession from Pakistan.

The Catholic diocese of Rawalpindi/Islamabad also experienced augmentation due to migration of Christians from other areas. Catholic housing colonies in towns provided for the resettlement of Christians from rural areas.[21] In the aftermath of independence and two wars with India the Christian population of Islamabad/Rawalpindi is said to have increased twofold between 1946 and 1986.[22]

Christian villages

Bishop Malik told me that in the Panjab you can walk into any village and you will find five to fifty families who are Christian. But still more interesting is the existence of all-Christian villages. According to the bishop there are two dozen exclusively Christian villages, such as Martinpur and Youngsonabad (clearly named after Youngson, the missionary). In 1898 Catholic and Protestant missionaries persuaded the British Government to allot to Christians land in newly irrigated areas known as 'Canal Colonies'. The Christians selected for land ownership had some experience of agriculture, not as landowners but mostly as agricultural labourers. These people, though of the same caste as the Chuhras, were called Kammis. On acquiring landownership, a prestigious position in the subcontinent, they became equivalent to Zamindars and began to claim that they were Jats or Rajputs. Self-appointed caste status is not unheard of in India, for instance many Muslims categorise themselves as Sayyid or Ashraf, descendants of the Prophet. Thus Christians in these Canal Colonies were able to achieve social mobility. It is probable that on acquiring higher social status they intermarried with higher castes. Linda Walbridge informs that many of the Canal Colony Christians do not look physically like the Chuhras, who are generally small-built and dark.[23]

In the early 1960s the Government of Pakistan embarked on a scheme to bring under cultivation large tracts of land on the eastern banks of the Indus (Sindhu). The church saw this as a good opportunity for Christians to settle down in a viable agricultural enterprise. Thus Christians settled on about 10, 000 acres of land. Canals

---

20 Rooney, *Symphony on Sands*, p. 104.

21 Rooney, John, *On Rocky Ground* (Rawalpindi,1987), p. 156.

22 Ibid., p. 147.

23 Walbridge, pp. 18-19.

were dug and roads built and tractors supplied with the price received for the land. The church formed an association called JADA (acronym for Jati Agricultural Development Association) and aid was forthcoming from abroad for the project.

However, the scheme was not an unqualified success due to the high salinity of the water available. The land allotted to the Christians was particularly so and many of the settlers had to leave. Some determined individuals stayed on, struggling to make a living. About 3000 acres of land are still in Christian hands.[24]

The history so far of Christianity in Pakistan shows that it was serial, ups and downs, and not a consistent or static saga. The original community avowedly established by St Thomas the Apostle and later under the domain of the Church of Persia had disappeared entirely by the sixteenth century, probably due to the ascendancy of Buddhism in the area. It was much later in the nineteenth century that the Missionary movements in Europe and America ventured into the Indian subcontinent, facilitated by the Empire under the British Crown, that there was a revival of Christianity in the area. These Christians mainly belonged to the stigmatised lower echelons of society, and could be seen as a struggling community socially and economically, unlike their co-religionists in, for instance, South India. National Independence, the formation of Pakistan, the wars with India and the declaration of an Islamic state in Pakistan were not circumstances to the advantage of the Christians. Christians in Pakistan are beset by many problems as a religious minority in an Islamic state, and I will deal in detail with these issues in subsequent chapters. However, the Christian community remains a lively and active community contending energetically with adverse circumstances and seeking to make their voice heard in the nation.

---

24 Rooney, *Symphony on Sands*, pp. 95-6.

Chapter Three

The Islamicisation of Pakistan

Throughout this monograph I have coined the term 'Islamicisation' and used it in preference to the term 'Islamisation'. This is because the words 'Islamism' and 'Islamisation' have acquired certain pejorative connotations in modern writings about Islam.

Islam came to the Pakistan region of the Indian subcontinent initially through invaders and later through the work of itinerant Sufi mystics. Not all of the conversions can be attributed to the sword. As a matter of fact, the very first invader, the 17-year-old Muslim General Muhammad ibn al Quasim, in 711-712 CE let most of the population of Sind remain in the Buddhist faith to which they belonged. Muhammad of Ghazna, the second Muslim invader, from Afghanistan, did carry out forced conversion of Indians to Islam, and was particularity notorious for his destruction of the beautiful temple of Somanatha in Kathiawar. The Ghaznavids, following the Hanafi Madahab (school of law) which still remains normative in Islam of the northern Indian Subcontinent, were from Afghanistan. Muhammad Ghori who also descended from Afghanistan was the next invader who extracted *jizyah* (a special tax for non-Muslims) from Hindus but also attracted many Hindus to Islam who wanted to escape the clutches of caste-based discrimination.

The impact of Sufism was also important. Sufism, in comparison to orthodox Islam, is flexible and adapted well to local faiths and culture, and therefore paved an easier way for Hindus to convert to Islam. The great al Hallaj, the first martyr of Sufism, was said to have visited Sind in 905 CE. Abu al As-Sindi and Ali al Hujwri are said to be other Sufi mystics who propagated their thinking in the Pakistan region. The latter is regarded as the first Sufi saint of Lahore under the name Data Ganj Baksh.[1]

I have already pointed out in the introductory chapter that Pakistan was never envisaged as an Islamic theocratic state by its founders. Both Allama Iqbal and Muhammad Ali Jinnah, the ideologues of the new state, had made it clear right from the outset.[2] Jinnah clarified his understanding of the two nation theory as follows at the All India Muslim League session in Lahore of 1940:

> They (Islam and Hinduism) are not religions in the strict sense of the word, but are, in fact, different and distinct social orders…. The Hindus and the Muslims belong to two different social philosophies, social customs and literature…and indeed they belong to two different civilizations, which are based mainly on conflicting ideas and conceptions….[3]

---

1   Schimmel, Annemarie, *Islam in the Indian Subcontinent* (Leiden-Koln, 1980), p. 8.
2   Iqbal, Afzal, *Islamicisation of Pakistan* (Delhi, 1984), p. 21.
3   Raza, Rafi (ed.), *Pakistan in Perspective*, 1947-1997 (Oxford, 1997), p. xviii.

It is clear from Jinnah's statement that it was not Islam as a religion that was the driving force behind his demand for dividing India. It is however ironic that he should look upon them as two conflicting civilizations, which is exactly the argument offered in modern times against Islam by some scholars and Western politicians as the source of the present political problems involving Islamic nations and organisations. However, history has proved that Jinnah is correct in implying Islam was not the binding force for national identity of Pakistan that everyone thought that it would be. Bangladesh was to separate from its eastern Muslim compatriots and Jinnah's thesis of cultural disparities did prove to be a force over-riding religious conformity.

The first Prime Minister of Pakistan, Liaquat Ali Khan, corroborated Jinnah's conception of Pakistan. He stated,

> I just now said that the people are the real recipients of power. This naturally eliminates any danger of the establishment of theocracy... which has come to mean a government by ordained priests, who wield authority as being specially appointed.... I cannot over-emphasise the fact that such an idea is absolutely foreign to Islam...and therefore the question of a theocracy simply does not arise in Islam.[4]

It is interesting that while conforming to Jinnah's ideology of Pakistan there are certain inaccuracies in Liaquat Ali Khan's statement. A theocracy need not necessarily mean rule by ordained priests. *Shura* – consultation between the ruler and the ruled, is an important requirement of an Islamic state. Moreover, it is well known there are no ordained priests in Islam. The Prime Minster is here probably referring to a body of Ulama acting as a consultative council, the equivalent of a Parliament in an Islamic state. In addition, to say that there is no theocracy in Islam is too sweeping a statement. The early history of Islam makes it clear that the Islamic state constituted in Medina and elsewhere operated under God's command. Islam is not necessary antithetical to a theocracy. The fundamental principle in an Islamic state is merely that the authority of the ruler, whether democratically elected or a dynastical monarch or an acclaimed religious leader, is delegated to him/her by God. In short, God is the paramount ruler of an Islamic state.

However, it is clear that what both Jinnah and Liaquat Ali Khan envisaged of Pakistan seems to be a secular democratic state rather than an Islamic state, as it is classically known. Secular not in the sense that it is inimical to religion or discouraged religious belief or practice, but that the state is even-handed in its treatment of all religious communities, and religious identity will not be a factor in the rights and treatment of the people. This envisages prefect freedom to worship, or even to propagate one's religion.

The fact is that many Muslims all over the world looked upon Pakistan with eager expectation as a blossoming model of an Islamic state. This included many Pakistani Muslims, Maulana Abul ala Mowdudi being a prime example. However, this was contrary to the designs of its founders and disappointment was to follow. The Islamic state that they envisaged was one which linked Islam and the state together, a Wahabi model of Islam, not the experiential and spiritual Islam of the Sufis who had initially spread Islam in the subcontinent. But their dreams were quickly shattered

---

4   Ibid., p. 29.

when the state modelled itself on a Western nation-state rather than Islamic traditions and political, educational, economic and legal systems. This disillusionment and the rampant corruption, mismanagement of funds, and continuing poverty in the nation set the stage for an Islamicisation venture that was not slow in coming. President Zia made political capital out of the frustration of the Pakistanis and the Islamic fundamentalists there in particular.

The liberal stance of Jinnah and Liaquat Ali Khan was steadily compromised in ensuing years. Though in the Objectives Resolution of 1949 non-Muslim citizens were guaranteed fundamental rights on a par with Muslim citizens, in the very first constitution passed in 1956 the state was given the name 'Islamic Republic of Pakistan'. Moreover, only a Muslim was eligible to become President of the nation. The constitution also stipulated that within one year the President should appoint a commission to bring all existing laws of the nation into conformity with Islamic principles. By the time the constitution of 1973 was implemented Islam was declared as the state religion of the country.[5] It also stipulated that the Prime Minister of the country should also be a Muslim. The oath of taking office of both the President and the Prime Minister now had words to the effect that they were Muslims and would believe in the fundamental tenets of the Islamic faith including the requirements and teachings of the Qur'an and the Sunnah. The Islamicisation of the state was thus escalating rapidly.

Prime Minister Zulfikar Ali Bhutto was a liberal Muslim who took an enlightened stand on the issue of Islam and the rights and status of religious minorities of Pakistan. Like Jinnah he was a Western-educated politician and must have imbibed a different sort of ideals and mindset from other leaders of Pakistan. He came to power in 1973 and oversaw the affairs of Pakistan until he was deposed by a military coup led by General Zia ul Haqq in 1977. Bhutto was a moderate in religious matters and did not use Islam as a major reform programme. It was never the key to his policy as in the case of his successor Zia. However, Bhutto in the end had to use Islam to bolster his position that was becoming shaky. The problems faced by the country were huge, and though he was optimistic in tackling these, ultimately he failed. He had entered politics as the champion of the dispossessed but he failed to deliver what he promised – *roti, kapada and makan,* (bread, cloth and shelter) the basic necessities of life to the masses of Pakistan. He was an astute politician and well knew that Islam could be a binding force and that a demagogue like himself could use the emotionality that Islam could arouse in the minds of the majority community. But he turned to Islam only as a last resort. Nevertheless, it did harm to the religious neutrality and avowed secular nature of the nation and consequently to the status of religious minorities. Bhutto however did not propose any radical Islamicisation of constitutional provisions or the law.

Islamicisation of Pakistan reached its peak during the reign of Zia ul Haqq, Martial Law Administrator from 1977 to 1988. It is a paradox that under the previous martial law administrators, Generals Ayyoub and Yahya Khan, the Islamicisation fervour had died down temporarily. Ayyoub even had the title 'Islamic' dropped from the

---

5   Afzal, p. 84.

name of the Republic.[6] It has to be remembered that Zia's reforms did not involve any democratic process. They were mainly the result of a fiat of the General's will. The Jamati Islami (Muslim League) was greatly encouraged by the Martial Law Administrator to act as a counter to Bhutto's Pakistan People's Party (PPP). Muslim Ulama joined the governing institutions of the nation in August 1978, their first taste of power, avoiding the usual constitutional processes.[7] This is a feature of the concept of the Islamic state as defined by Muslim ideologues of the Islamic State. The Shura (Consultative Body or Parliament) of the Islamic State should be composed not of elected representatives from the citizenry but of Ulama. Thus Zia seems to have been carrying out this principle of the classical ideology of the Islamic State.

Under Zia the principles and provisions of the preamble became an integral part of the constitution thereby according it a legal authority it had not possessed so far. By making the Objective Resolutions a substantive part of the Constitution he vested the Islamicisation of Pakistan with a legal validity and authority it had not enjoyed in the preamble. A Federal Shari'a Court was established under a new Chapter 3A of the constitution mainly to examine and decide upon the Islamic credentials of existing laws and legal provisions. Appeals from this court were to be heard by the Supreme Court, but only by an appellate bench of the Court consisting of Muslim judges, and not only judges who were Muslim, but also two Ulama, religious scholars. Raza opines that such benches could very well have been set up in all High Courts, obviating the necessity of a Federal Shari'a court.[8] But this Court was a visible symbol of Zia's Islamicisation programme and hence essential to his policy. The court had powers to examine laws made by Parliament and whether they conformed to the principles of Islamic law. This implies an authority over-riding even Parliament, the highest seat of power in the land. Zia introduced separate electorates for non-Muslims, a fact I have already mentioned in Chapter 1 as one which aroused the ire of Bishop Malik, the Moderator of the Church of Pakistan, who did not use his franchise until this sectarian provision was abrogated.

Another reform was that Muslim Members of Parliament should be subject to a more rigorous moral life. He/she should not be 'commonly known as one who violates Islamic injunctions, and should have adequate knowledge of Islamic teachings and practices and obligatory duties prescribed by Islam as well as abstains from major sins (sic)'.[9]

It is said that the Zia administration encouraged Islamic militancy, a travesty of the intentions of the founding fathers of the nation. It is said that members of the Sipahi-I-Sahaba and Jaish-I-Muhammad marched in public with lethal weapons.[10] The Enforcement of Shari'a Act 1991 apparently provides for Islamicisation of Education (Sec 7), Islamicisation of Economy (Sec 8), the Islamicisation of Mass Media (Sec 9) and the Islamicisation of the Judicial System (Sec 14). It is evident all these are spheres which should support neutrality and equality of the citizens of the

---

6   Raza, Rafi, p. 29.
7   See Afzal, p. 107.
8   Raza, Rafi, p. 37
9   Ibid.
10 Mentioned in *The Christian Voice* (20 June 2004): 116.

state, irrespective of religious affiliation. Clause 1 of Section 7 states that: 'The State shall take necessary steps to ensure that the educational system of Pakistan is based on Islamic values of learning, teaching and character building.' This injunction does not consider how such an educational system will affect non-Muslim citizens of the state. I will in another section examine the matter of education more closely. Clause 4 of Section 8 stipulates the objective that: 'The Commission shall oversee the process of elimination of *riba* (interest) from every sphere of economic activity in the shortest possible time and also recommend such measures to the Government as would ensure the total elimination of *riba* from the economy.' It is incomprehensible how this can be achieved in a modern economy that cannot work in isolation from the economies of non-Muslim countries. The fact is that in spite of the stipulation to achieve the elimination of *riba* in the shortest possible time it is still extant in Pakistan 14 years after the promulgation of the act.

Section 16 makes a blanket provision for Islamicisation of Pakistan: 'The State shall enact laws to protect the ideology, solidarity and integrity of Pakistan as an Islamic State'. The exhortation to solidarity and integrity as an Islamic state seems to exclude minority faiths and compromise their status as full fledged citizens and an integral part of the nation.

Islamicisation of the legal system

Though the Supreme Court had validated General Zia Ul Haqq's imposition of martial law in view of a national crisis after the election of 1977, in March 1977 the General had given a solemn promise that the suspension of the 1973 constitution would last only up to October and that fair and free elections would be organised then, that the suspended constitution would be restored and power transferred to elected representatives. However, this came about only after the General's death in a mysterious air crash in August 1988. In the intervening years he amended the suspended constitution several times without any popular mandate. The provisional constitutional order promulgated by him in 1981 dealt a severe blow to the judiciary by which their powers, including that of the Supreme Court, were curtailed. The establishment of a Federal Shari'a Court was a major amendment to the constitution and it was an integral part of Zia's Islamicisation programme. Islamicisation of the state was also strengthened by making the Objectives Resolution a substantive part of the constitution rather than merely a part of the preamble.

The Council of Islamic Ideology was instituted to ensure that all laws enacted in the nation are conformable to the principles of Islam and the Shari'a. It can make recommendations for the amendment of laws to Parliament in order to achieve the Islamicisation of the legal system in Pakistan. It has no non-Muslim representation in its ranks and does not consider the sentiments and interests of non-Muslims in its recommendations. This is extremely counter-productive for good inter-religious relations in a religiously pluralistic society and might easily undermine the rights and status of non-Muslims. It is imperative that such an organisation should not suppress the religious minority voices, but should listen to them in order that no section of society would be undermined by its recommendations. It is unjust that though the council does not have any non-Muslim representation its expenditure is borne by the whole nation.[11] I.A. Rahim is wholly right in stating that the laws of Pakistan relate only to the religious sentiments of the Muslim citizens of Pakistan.[12]

These reforms were not without protest by the judiciary. When judges were asked to take an oath to uphold these amendments which necessarily restricted their powers, 19 judges declined to do so and were removed from office arbitrarily. It is evident that the powers of the judiciary to decide whether legislation was valid were of little account in the system. All litigation regarding the legitimacy of Zia's rule was also set aside. The rule of law, the basic premise of an orderly democratic society and often the final resort against injustice in nations, was therefore effectively compromised. Zia's avowed statement was 'The Islamic political system does not envisage majority rule'.[13] The cornerstone of democracy, the will of the majority, was thus declared null and void. Zia seems to be stating that in a purely Islamic state opposition to the government is untenable since such opposition is tantamount to opposition to the divine order.

A dubious referendum was conducted on 19 December 1984 to impart some validity for Zia's Islamicisation of the state and the legal system. The referendum asked only one question:

Do you endorse the process initiated by General Muhammad Zia ul Haqq, President of Pakistan, for bringing the laws of Pakistan into conformity with the injunctions of Islam as laid down in the Holy Qur'an and the Sunnah of the Holy Prophet (PBUH) and for the preservation of the Islamic ideology of Pakistan, the continuation and consolidation of that process, and for a smooth and orderly transfer of power to the elected representatives of the people?[14]

It is clear that this question does not give much leeway for giving a negative answer to the referendum since that would immediately be construed as disrespect for the Qur'an, Prophet Muhammad and Islam. On 15 June 1988 Zia declared through an ordinance the Shari'a as the supreme law of the land. Accordingly Ulama could be appointed as judges of any court and could challenge all existing laws of the nation.

Under this system the status and experience of religious minorities such as Christians became extremely vulnerable. Abdul Sattar Ghazzali opines that the citizens of Pakistan under this suppression and distortion of the political process became not Pakistanis but members of various *biraderi*, or tribes or religious sects.[15] No wonder that the US State Department in its annual report for 1985 surmised that

---

11 *The Christian Voice* (25 July 2004): 4.

12 Rahim, I.A., 'A critique of Pakistan's blasphemy laws', in Tarik, Jan (ed.), *Pakistan between Secularism, and Islam* (Islamabad, 1998), pp. 195-207, p. 201.

13 Quoted by Ghazali, Abdus Sattar in *Pakistan: Illusions and Reality* (Islamabad, 1996), p. 24.

14 Quoted in Ibid., p. 124

15 Ibid, p. 239.

in Pakistan Hindus, Christians and Parsis do not enjoy the same rights as Muslims[16] – a clear indictment of the unfairness of Zia's political and legal reforms.

Islamicisation of education

Pakistan's Islamic schools or Madrassas have come under the spotlight when allegations were made in the international press that they were breeding grounds for militancy and terrorists such as suicide bombers. How legitimate these claims are is not clear. Not all Madrassas are ideologically similar in orientation, and therefore generalisations that they are brainwashing youngsters into hardliners may not be valid. President Pervez Musharaff even declared that he would bring them under state control and into mainstream education by the end of 2006, but eventually shied away from it, no doubt fearing a fundamentalist backlash. The President needs the support of the Muttahida Majlis Amal, the umbrella organisation of Islamic religiously oriented political parties. Zia had encouraged the Jamat I Islami (Muslim League) as a deterrent to the PPP and during his regime the Islamic parties were in the ascendancy. Their significance and influence have not disappeared even now.

Educational methods in the Madrassas are outdated and crude. Rote learning of texts is very common and the Ulama taught by creating an atmosphere of fear that managed to persuade students to work hard. But there was also a core of students who were committed to the study of Islam, and the Taliban for example were products of such Madrassas in the North West frontier with Afghanistan. The Sub-Editor of *The Dawn* whom I interviewed had a class and economic interpretation of education. According to him there are three tiers of education, the lower middle class send their children to the Madrassas, the middle class to public sector schools and the upper middle class to English medium British style schools, perhaps those managed by Christian institutions. It is clear that the choice of school depends on the level of fees charged by the school. The British GCSE/A level type of school would be the most expensive and the Madrassas the cheapest. According to the Editor those who are inclined to religion do not send their children to the English medium public school type of institutions. Butler and Chagathai point out that many Muslim parents think that in spite of the education of a good standard that they impart their children are exposed to Westernisation in the public school type of institutions, and this tends to erode their Islamic beliefs and culture.[17] It may be that the lower two tiers of schools are the ones where the children are most exposed to Islam. So the choice of school would be dictated by both the economic capability of the parents and their commitment to Islamic nurture of their children.

The Madrassas might also be the only place where Pakistani children receive Islamic religious nurture. The syllabi of these schools are particularly designed to give instruction in Arabic, study of the Qur'an, Hadith, life of the Prophet and Islamic rituals. In some countries children have to attend the Madrassas as well as secular schools. But in Pakistan all schools have to teach Islamiyyat. This subject

---

16 Ibid., p. 135.
17 Butler, Robert A., and Chagathai, M. Ikram, *Trying to Respond* (Lahore, 1994), p. 329.

is compulsory for all children up to grade eight but from grade nine non-Muslims can opt out by choosing Civics. Bishop Malik told me, however, that Muslim teachers recognise that those who opt for Civics are non-Muslims and they might be marked down in assessment. He personally encouraged Christian children to study Islamiyyat since they then would have an authentic knowledge of Islam and be more well informed and tolerant of their Muslim compatriots, with the added benefit of getting better marks than if they had opted for Civics. Mrs Imtiaz, wife of a vicar, told me that children in Grade One are asked questions such as 'Who are we?' to which the answer should be 'We are Muslims', and 'What is a place of worship?' answered by 'It is a Masjid'. Children have to learn these answers by rote whatever their religion might be. It is apparent that the teaching in classes does not take into account the religious diversity of Pakistan, and would hurt the feelings of religious minorities. It is as though their existence in the state is completely ignored. It of course conforms to the notion that Pakistan is an Islamic state, and that Islam defines Pakistani identity and citizenship. Such coalescence of Islam and national identity is, however, counter-productive to non-Muslim citizens as they feel themselves to be aliens in their own country and relegated to the ranks of *dhimmi* or second class citizens, almost an unwanted intrusion into the body politic.

Bishop Azariah of the Raiwind Church of Pakistan Diocese reiterated Mrs Imtiaz's statement. To him as to Bishop Malik the teaching of Islamiyyat is not very much of a problem. They even welcome the study of other religions by Christians. But Islamic chauvinism has infiltrated other subjects also – even secular subjects such as Geography and History. Subjects such as History are obviously subject to interpretation, but if the interpretation is heavily biased in favour of Islam it does not lead us to the avowed objective of all education and research – arriving at the truth. For example, if in Geography the question is asked, 'Who lives in Pakistan?' and the reply expected and taught is 'Muslims' it is certainly not a valid answer. Similarly to the question 'Who founded Pakistan?' the answer taught is again 'Muslims' – though obviously Christians and Hindus had a definite part to play in the freedom struggle against the colonial regime in India. 'Whom does Pakistan belong to?' the answer taught is 'Muslims'. This is chilling for non-Muslim Pakistanis. It is almost as if they are rejected as citizens of Pakistan. This answer must certainly generate a feeling of alienation from Pakistani society. If Pakistan belongs to Muslims what rights can non-Muslims have? Their very existence is threatened. If this is what Pakistani children learn in schools how can there be religious harmony in the nation? The Qur'an advocates religious tolerance – 'To you your religion; to me mine', and 'There is no compulsion in religion' (Qur'an 2:256). These verses indicate clearly that God/Allah is against religious chauvinism and discrimination.

According to Bishop Azariah even at higher levels of education the teaching about Christianity is negative. The main historical issue highlighted is the Crusades and secondly the colonial era, both of which do not depict Christians in a favourable light. Why not teach also more positive issues such as the Ethiopian Christian king, the Negus, who gave refuge to the early Muslims from persecution by the Quraish, or Islamic Spain where Christians and Muslims subsisted in harmony and cooperation in what is considered as the Golden Age of Spain? Or the close doctrinal and historical affinities between the two faiths, and the centrality of Jesus in both the Qur'an and the Bible?

Christian schools and colleges are very popular in Pakistan. The education they impart is said to be of a better standard than many state-run schools. Bishop Malik told me that many of the leaders of Pakistan are products of Christian schools. Butler and Chagathai point out that the work of nuns in colleges and schools is very much appreciated by Muslim students and parents.[18] They say that the majority of students in Christian schools are Muslim and in reality only one per cent of their students are Christians.[19] This strikingly testifies to the popularity of Christian schools among all Pakistanis. It is even said that a Christian head of college took initiative in Christian-Muslim rapprochement such as the celebration of Mawlid un Nabi (Birth anniversary of the Prophet) in her college.[20] Muslims are very much sensitive about respect to the Prophet and this nun's move was highly appreciated by Muslim students and parents. But the Islamic bias is not obviated by the Christian management since the textbooks used are prescribed by the state and continue the aforementioned anomalies.

Points of critique against Christian schools are that they are hotbeds of alien ideology and that they cater only to the well-to-do classes. Many Pakistanis feel that the West still has a crusader complex and has a mission to destroy Islam. They tend to associate Christian schools particularly with this hidden agenda, since they have a missionary foundation and are likely to have anti-Islamic designs to destroy the purity of Islam.

It is obvious that these allegations are mostly unwarranted as far as Christian schools and colleges in India and Pakistan are concerned. Many are places where the poor are welcomed. Christian schools are doing their best to indigenise and measures taken to conform to the local culture. There is also nowadays no overt evangelising agenda, though the school might have a Christian ethos in general. Even this is very muted; the morning assembly for instance no longer has a Christian focus.

But the anti-Western paranoia of some Pakistani Muslims is quite apparent, especially after the Afghan and Iraqi wars. Even Western scholarly publications on Islam are distrusted. They might be looked upon as designed to undermine faith in Islam by opening up to critical analysis matters that are held as fundamental truth in Islam. Muslim scholars who are perceived as liberal and susceptible to Western positions in the study of Islam are also suspect. Fazlur Rahman, a liberal Islamic scholar who advocates openness and reform in contrast to orthodox Islamic inflexibility, for instance, was forced to resign in 1968 from the Government-sponsored Central Institute of Islamic Research. Indeed he is no longer in Pakistan. Initiatives in Christian-Muslim dialogue are also viewed with suspicion by some Muslims as an evangelistic device. Interestingly, I saw that the Christian Study Centre in Rawalpindi, which is a dialogue-oriented institution used by both Muslim and Christian scholars, had no signboard and was guarded by an armed policeman who let in visitors only after careful scrutiny. This indicated that the management

---

18 Ibid.
19 Ibid.
20 Ibid., p. 32.

was not entirely certain that as a centre devoted to promoting good Christian-Muslim relations it is entirely safe from attack by Islamic militants.

Islamicisation of politics

I have already mentioned that during General Zia's regime many fundamentalist ulama joined the administration without going through the electoral process. In August 1978 the Jamat I Islami joined the Zia al Haqq government, their first taste of power in Pakistan. This was a total contradiction of the principles and aspirations of the founders of Pakistan. Afzal Iqbal opines that this could never have happened through a constitutional process.[21] Zia seems to have appropriated into the state the powers of religious institutions. Mumtaz Ahmed points out that the emphasis of Islamicisation was on the Shari'a and strengthening of the Islamic character of the state rather than on freedom, equality and social justice.[22] Indeed, in the Islamicisation quest in religiously pluralistic Pakistan these important objectives of any democratic system seem to have been undermined. Anyway, the problem with martial law regimes is that the suspension of political parties creates a vacuum in which fissiparous tendencies based on religion, ethnicity and such sectarian matters tend to emerge. Even elsewhere in the subcontinent there is a tendency for politics to be identified with caste, religion and ethnicity, rather than general ideologies such as Capitalism or Marxism. The position of minorities becomes highly vulnerable in such a scenario. It is possible to change one's ideological stance, so the numbers in ideologically based parties are always in a flux. However, it is not possible to change one's political affiliation so easily, if it is based on religion, caste or ethnicity. The Christians of Pakistan are naturally excluded from organisations such as the Jamat I Islami since it requires an Islamic identity to be a member. Mumtaz Ahmed opines that a theocratic state is sectarian by definition, and large sections of people will lose their political freedom and even religious rights.[23]

As a matter of fact, in spite of Zia's intensive Islamicisation programme Pakistan has not become a full-fledged theocratic state. Its political institutions are still largely secular. The traditions are based on Westminster, not Mecca and Medina. Even this democratic system has been suspended on and off to make way for martial law administrations. In my interview with him Imran Khan, leader of Tareekh Insaaf (Justice Party) opined that Pakistan has never had a true democracy.

The Islamic state is still one in which there is consultation (*shura*) between the ruler and the ruled. But in the classical concept of an Islamic state the representatives of the people are Islamic scholars. A legislative body of Ulama is the only valid form of law-making agency in such a state. The head of government will be one who is well versed in fiqh. These criteria are fulfilled in only one state in the world – Iran. There, though there are elected representatives in the Majlis e Shura e Islami

---

21 Iqbal, p. 107.

22 Ibid.

23 Ahmad, Mumtaz, 'Revivalism, Islamisation, sectarianism and violence in Pakistan', in Baxter, C. and Kennedy, C.H. (eds), *Pakistan 2000* (Westview Press, 1998), pp. 101-21, p. 128.

their legislation has to be reviewed by a Council of Guardians, composed of six religious members appointed by the Supreme Leader and six lay members all of whom are lawyers. The Supreme Leader who has an overriding authority on all levels of government is a religious scholar, notably on *fiqh*, religious law. It is clear that there cannot be a tenable opposition in the classical form of an Islamic State. Opposition to the ruler could be construed as opposition to God since in the Islamic state ultimately governance lies in the hand of God/Allah, the authority of the human ruler being merely a delegated authority. The Pakistan constitution states:

> To God almighty belongs sovereignty over the whole universe and the authority delegated to the State of Pakistan through its people is to be exercised within the limits prescribed by Him.

Fazlur Rahman cogently opined: 'Islam is made a limiting concept rather than a creative factor'.[24]

However, the constitution also states that: 'Adequate provisions (sic) will be made for the minorities freely to profess and practise their religions and develop their cultures'. In Zia's constitutional amendments the word 'freely' was omitted from this clause.[25]

In Pakistan the Islamic Council of Ideology has the task of ensuring that all legislation conforms to the principles of the Shari'a, which in turn derives essentially from the Qur'an and the Hadith. However, the nature of the state in Pakistan is not the same as that of the classical definition of the Islamic state. Joshua Fazl-ud-din opines that the very idea of federation is against the concept of the Islamic state.[26] It will be difficult to ensure that all legislation in the different provinces will conform to the stipulations of the Shari'a. This condition can only form the general principle of law making and governance in Pakistan. This is clearly set out in Para C of the Objectives Resolution which has now become a substantive part of the constitution rather than merely in the Preamble: 'Wherein the Muslims shall be enabled to order their lives, in their individual and collective spheres, in accord with the teachings of Islam as set out in the Holy Qur'an and the Sunnah'.

Mawdudi, the great Muslim ideologue of the Indian Subcontinent once stated that: 'The Islamic state is an ideological state rather different from a national state. Non-Muslims cannot participate in policy making in such a state, only in administration'.[27] Even Liaquat Ali Khan, the first Prime Minister of Pakistan who was avowedly committed to secularism, had pledged 'The state will create such conditions as are conducive to the building up of a truly Islamic society, which means that the state will have to play a positive part in this effort'.[28] However, no one other than General Zia had taken this principle literally and tried to implement it whole-heartedly. The fact is that while the Muslim citizens of Pakistan respect and cherish Islam and its

---

24 Quoted in Butler and Chagatai, p. 337.

25 20. Shakir, Naeem, 'The state of religious freedom in Pakistan', in '*Al-Mushir*, 45/4 (2003): 109-26, 115.

26 Fazl-ud-din, Joshua, *The Future of Christians in Pakistan* (Lahore, 1949), p. 84.

27 Quoted in Butler and Chagatai, p. 338.

28 Quoted in Fazl-ud-din, Joshua, p. 92.

values, they do not want to hand over their nation to the rule of Ulama, but would like to be governed under a more or less secular structure as envisioned in contemporary universal thought. Many Muslims state: Islam is all right and we must have it; but we do not want it forced down our throats.[29] It is apparent that the fundamentalists in Pakistan are not in a majority. However, they are a vociferous community who make their demands known in such a concerted manner that no politician, however liberal minded, can ignore them.

However, in a religiously pluralistic society such as that of Pakistan only a secular mode of government will ensure equality and justice to citizens of all faiths. The alternative will be to class certain citizens such as the Christians as *ahl al dhimma* (protected citizens). This entails paying a special tax, the *Jizyah* (a poll tax) and the *Kharaj* (a land tax). Liabilities would be that the dhimmi are subject to certain restrictions such as not building new houses of worship or even repairing old ones, not worshipping in the open, not preaching or performing rituals of their religion in public, not dressing like Muslims, not publishing or disseminating religious literature. They cannot be members of the shura (consultative councils). On the positive side dhimmi are accorded all freedom in worship (in private), they are ensured of protection of life, wealth and honour, they are allowed to work and trade. Then they are exempt from paying zakat (the almsgiving of one-twentieth of savings obligatory on Muslims) from compulsory military service, and from Islamic rituals.[30]

These conditions show that the *ahl al dhimma* are not eligible for equal status with Muslims in an Islamic state. This is why Bishop Malik stated that he had no objection to Pakistan being called an Islamic Republic as long as that name does not have the connotation of the traditional Islamic states of the Middle East. But Butler and Chagathai opine that many non-Muslims would be happier if the ideal and objective of an Islamic state was abandoned by Pakistan.[31] While Christians are accorded freedom of worship, Bishop Malik has a grievance that they found it difficult to obtain wine for the Eucharist, which he construed as restricting and interfering with their freedom of worship. In 1977 the Prime Minister had given into opposition demands and changed the weekly holiday from Sunday to Friday, quite a legitimate action in view of the fact that Muslims formed the majority of the population, but he also banned the sale of liquor, a salutary measure for public health and morality no doubt, but putting Christian performance of the Eucharist in jeopardy.

The *ahl al dhimma* were originally conceived as a conquered people, but the Christian and Hindu etc. citizens of Pakistan were not conquered by Muslims. They just happened to be in the Pakistan region of the Indian subcontinent when Pakistan was carved out of British India in August 1947. As Bishop Malik stated, the Christians and other religious minorities also had a role in the creation of Pakistan by campaigning against colonial rule. But the Bishop is apprehensive that if the Ulama came to power in parliament they might try to create a *dhimmi* role for religious

---

29 Quoted in Butler and Chagathai, p. 346.

30 http://en.wikipedia.org/wiki/Dhimmi.

31 Butler and Chagathai, p. 343.

minorities. Indeed the question of *Jizyah* for religious minorities had been raised now and then, once by a Minister for Religious Affairs.[32]

Part of the problem is that non-Muslims may be considered by the majority community to be lacking in loyalty to the state of Pakistan. This is a notion that is held even by moderate Muslims.[33] The reasons for this misconception are complex. If national identity coalesces with religious identity as tends to happen in Pakistan, i.e. national identity tends to be that of Islam since the Muslims are in a vast majority, then religious minorities may be thought of as lacking in affinity to national interests, especially in times of war. If national identity is defined by birth or even long and permanent residence in a geographical territory that delineates national boundaries, then the suspicion of disloyalty or lack of commitment to the nation does not arise, since all citizens are expected to have such interests at heart, even though traitors to a nation among its citizenry are not unheard of. But to class an entire religious community or communities as disloyal to a nation leads to horrendous problems. In that case the community whose patriotism is questioned becomes anathema to the majority community, especially if an enemy nation is also defined, often erroneously, in religious terms. Inter-religious relations can be entirely jeopardised in such a situation. The religious minorities can be victimised and vulnerable even to physical violence. It will lead to an intolerable situation for them especially in times of war. The Hindus of Pakistan and even the *Muhajjirun* (Muslim migrants from India) might have found themselves in a delicate and problematic situation in times of war with India, and the Christians vulnerable in the present situation of Muslim hostility to the United States, Britain and other Western nations who are involved in the Iraq war.

Secondly, if in a foreign nation the majority of its citizens belong to a particular religion such as in a Christian United States or a Hindu India then the religious minorities belonging to these religions in Pakistan could be looked upon as more committed to these nations than to Pakistan. As a matter of fact in both nations cited national identity is not defined by religion since these are religiously pluralistic nations and the policy and constitution of these nations are even-handed to all religions. However, there can be a feeling among Muslim Pakistanis, as Bishop Azariah remarked, that the Christians of Pakistan are more loyal to the West than to Pakistan, since the West is often identified with the Christian faith. This is not an entirely valid proposition nowadays when secularism is in the ascendancy in the West, and Christianity has been on the decline there for long. This fallacious notion is held even more strongly by fundamentalists who belong to the majority religious community, though as I have mentioned earlier even moderate Muslims in Pakistan are said to be harbouring such erroneous conceptions. In the present situation, when the United States has been judged from its actions in Iraq and support of Israel to be anti-Muslim and to be a Christian power bent upon a crusade against Islam, such notions gather strength to the detriment of the Christian community of Pakistan.

Tarik Jan opines that the Islamic state is not necessarily adversarial to the civil society. She points out that the tension between law and individual freedoms or the

---

32 Ibid., p. 344.
33 Ibid., p. 341.

'never-ending conflict between societal good and individual rights' is mostly non-existent in an Islamic state.[34] This is because, she feels, that the Shari'a, contrary to man-made laws, is held sacrosanct both by the state and its subjects. Khomeini also in his conception of the Islamic state predicts that there will be no need for the police or any form of coercion on the citizens for submitting to law in an Islamic state, for the law will be revered by the populace and they will obey it voluntarily, since the Shari'a is God-given law, not of human provenance. He thought, I presume, that since infringement of the Shari'a is not only a crime but also a sin against God people will comply with such laws. But he would not have felt so sanguine in the light of his experiences when he became ruler of Iran.

On the other hand, Tarik Jan has a critique of secularism as national ideology. She states that the secular state decomposes religion as 'It empties God of His authority and upstages him as an inert being'. She is of the opinion that in a secular nation the state 'Arrogates to itself an extensive role from law making to adjudication and from education to cultural aspects', thus implying that the state is restricting or interfering with civil liberties. She states that the secular states replace God with an idolatry of the masses who 'combine in themselves the ruler as well as the ruled'.[35]

It is difficult to agree with Tarik Jan on this issue. In a secular state the law is flexible and the power still resides with the populace as it has a voice at least in the selection of law-making representatives if not in law-making itself. That the state has a voice in law-making and dispensing of justice and the education of its subjects is legitimate and even necessary, as otherwise the state might descend to chaos and anarchy. On the other hand the Shari'a and other religiously oriented law systems can be inflexible and outdated, not taking into consideration the present needs and changes in ethical views of the modern world. Many of modern phenomena such as genetics and information technology were not at all envisaged and provided for in medieval legal systems such as that of Islamic Law. And in a democracy the people are indeed both the ruler and the ruled, since democracy is government 'Of the people, by the people, and for the people'.

It is surprising that Pakistan did not take as model the ideology of Sir Sayyid Ahmad Khan, a great Muslim leader and ideologue of nineteenth century British India, who had a role in the formation of the Pakistan idea. That he is highly regarded in Pakistan is unquestionable. One of the country's universities, The Engineering and Technology University in Karachi, is named after him. Sir Sayyid was a person who championed Muslim–Christian dialogue – he even termed Jesus as the Sirdar (leader) of the Muslims as well as Christians and wrote a book on Christianity, called *Tabiun al Kalam*. Sayyid Ahmad Khan promoted modern technology and science and supported the idea of a Western-oriented education and progress for the Muslims of India, while at the same time being committed to Islam and Islamic sciences. His Anglo-Oriental Muhammadan College in Aligarh (now Aligarh Muslim University) was founded to promote such an ideology among Muslims of India at a time when the

---

34 Jan, Tarik, 'Questioning the Blasphemy Laws', pp. 241-56, in Jan, Tarik (ed.), *Pakistan between Secularism and Islam: Ideology, Issues and Conflict* (Islamabad, 1998), p. 243.

35 Jan, Tarik, Introduction, p. 8.

community was in the doldrums following the so-called Sepoy Mutiny of 1857, and the exile of the titular Mogul Emperor to Myanmar and imprisonment of hundreds of Muslims in the Andaman Islands. The fortunes of Muslims declined in British India due to their opposition to science, modern technology and English whereas the Hindus and Christians prospered and secured employment by qualifying in modern schools and colleges. Sir Sayyid sought to reverse this trend and was eventually immensely successful. Sayyid was a rationalist though a devout Muslim and had a radical hermeneutic that looked upon nature as God's handiwork, and science as studying God's creation. He was opposed to superstition and miracles as contrary to God's law in nature.

Sir Sayyid's paradigm could have been a better model for the prosperity and modernisation of Pakistan than the Mawdudi model which has only fostered fundamentalism, isolation from the world community and fractured inter-religious relations.

Islam has featured prominently in constitutional changes in Pakistan, especially during the Zia ul Haqq regime. In all debates, political, socio-economic and educational, Islam has been projected as the state ideology. This has had its consequences both for inter-religious harmony and the welfare of religious minorities such as the Christians and the Ahamadiyya. The Islamic fundamentalist organisations have been demanding strongly an Islam-based constitution and Shari'a-based legal system in the country. This demand has not been acceded to fully, especially by the Musharaff regime, since it is doubtful that there is public appetite for that sort of reform in the country. The present political situation in the Middle East has certainly fuelled such demands, and the secular and liberal opposition to the demands of the likes of the Muttahida Majlis Amal or the Jamat I Islami has been muted by the impolitic actions of Israel and President Bush of the USA. Mumtaz Ahmad points out that the military and civil oligarchy that rules Pakistan has only used Islam in a symbolic manner, for legitimising their political hegemony and supporting the social forces which are their power base.[36] The symbols include an Islamic penal code, some interest-free counters in banks, Shari'a courts, Islamic universities, chadors (full-length dress that veils the face and the body) for women employees and marathon Islamic conferences. But the political and economic status quo of poverty, economic and social deprivation and exploitation continues unameliorated by this superficial Islamicisation. Islam has become a tool for oppression, especially of the religious minorities, and a palliative for socially and economically deprived Muslim masses rather than an uplifting and ennobling force that it really should be. Mumtaz Ahmad also points out that the Islamic revivalism of the 1980s was primarily politicised, ideologist but non-pietist.[37] There is more than a germ of truth in this. The emphasis on Islamicisation seems to have been legalistic and symbolic rather than deep-rooted, spiritual and resulting in true *shura*, justice and individual freedom.

---

36 Ahmad, Mumtaz, p. 103.
37 Ibid., p. 106.

Chapter Four

The Christian dilemma: Problems faced by the Christian community of Pakistan

The issue of minorities in pluralistic democratic states is fraught with many problems. Most democracies know it is imperative to preserve the rights of minorities, for them to receive equal rights and treatment from the state, to preserve their religious and cultural identity, accord freedom to profess and practise their religion and customs, and at the same time enable them to participate fully in the political and economic life of the nation. The founders of Pakistan, Jinnah, Liaquat Ali Khan and Allama Iqbal also realised that this was the way forward, they termed it secularism, though that was not quite the appropriate word for their aspirations. However, the fact that Pakistan was created on the basis of religious identity, in this case Islam, very much complicates the nature of the new state formed. Pakistan was envisaged as a homeland for the Muslims of the Indian subcontinent, nevertheless it was not meant to be a theocratic state. However, there seemed to be an impending coalescence of national and religious identity, and future events proved that to be the case. The aftermath of an Islamic nationalism would be however to exclude the religious minorities from political, civic and economic processes, to marginalise them and lead to possible conflict and counter-nationalism, even culminating in secession. This did happen in the case of the Bengali ethnic element of Pakistan, leading to the secession of East Pakistan from the federation. The religious minorities are of course too small to demand secession or autonomy, but nevertheless if they are discriminated against or excluded from national affairs there is going to be dissatisfaction and a backlash that can be disruptive to the national life in addition to being unjust and not in conformity with universally accepted principles of equality and human rights. Article 27 of the United Nations International Covenant of Civil and Political Rights states:

> In those states in which ethnic, religious or linguistic minorities exist, persons belonging to such minorities shall not be denied the right in community with other members of their group, to enjoy their own culture, to profess and practise their own religion, or to use their own language.[1]

Minorities are often under pressure. If a particular group can identify themselves as a majority whether it be on the basis of race, ethnicity or religion they are likely to have feelings of superiority and to see the minorities as a distraction, as alien

---

1   Quoted in Thornberry, Patrick, 'International and European standards on minority rights', in Miall, Hugh, *Minority Rights in Europe* (London, 1994), pp. 14-21, p. 15.

and as troublemakers who are liable to undermine the state and their own welfare. This is evidently what happened to the Jews of Nazi Germany. There they were made the scapegoats for all the ills of the nation, the Nordic race was considered to be superior to the Semitic, and therefore to be preserved pure from contamination by alliance with the Jews who were looked upon as aliens, not co-citizens. The BNP, The National Front and such extreme right-wing parties in Britain and their counterparts in European states have similar feelings with regard to blacks and other ethnic groups in their midst. They may be looked upon as stealing the jobs of the group identified as the majority and as the true citizens of the state, so they have to be eliminated or deported from the land, however long they might have resided there or even if they are born in the land. A feeling of hostility can easily be built up towards them and they can be considered as a nuisance and even as undermining the welfare and status of the nation.

The gradual Islamicisation of Pakistan which saw an extraordinary escalation under Zia ul Haqq (1977-1988), and which has not effectively mitigated since, has caused the marginalisation of Christians and other religious minorities in the nation. Christians might be looked upon as aliens, when in fact they were in the Pakistan region even before the partition of British India. But to many Pakistani Muslims they are *persona non grata*, to be looked down upon and to be treated differently from themselves. At best they are to be assimilated by religious conversion and at worst expelled from the nation. Mumtaz Ahmad rightly remarks that under Zia the Islamicisation was Shari'atic, i.e. legalistic and the emphasis was not on democracy, freedom, equality or social justice.[2] This is highly counterproductive to the rights and status of religious minorities. Mumtaz points out also that a theocracy is by definition sectarian and large sections of people will lose their political freedom and even religious rights. As Fazlur Rahman opines, Islam was made a limiting concept rather than a creative factor.[3] Butler opines that the rights enjoyed by non-Muslims are thought to be those conferred by the Shari'a rather than fundamental rights.[4] So if eventually Pakistan becomes an Islamic state the plight of Christians will be even direr than it is now. Western intervention on behalf of human rights will be highly suspect in the present context due to the illegal war in Iraq and the killing of many innocent civilians there by Western forces. As Butler and Chagathai point out the West is misunderstood by many Pakistani Muslims to still possess a crusader complex. This weakens the power of Western states and organisations to intercede on behalf of the Christian and other minorities.

Jinnah in a speech in 1947 made clear that he was not in favour of a theocratic or Islamic state. He said:

> You may belong to any religion, caste or creed – that has nothing to do with the business of the state....We are starting in the days when there is no discrimination, no distinction between one community and another, no discrimination between one caste or creed or

---

2   Ahmed, Mumtaz, 'Revivalism, Islamisation, sectarianism and violence in Pakistan', in Bootes, Craig, and Kennedy, Charles, *Pakistan 1997*, (Colorado 1998), pp. 101-21, p. 107.

3   Quoted in Butler, Robert and Chagathai, M. Ikram, *Trying to Respond* (Lahore, 1994), p. 337.

4   Ibid., p. 339.

another. We are starting with this fundamental principle that we are all equal citizens of the one state.[5]

Though in the Objectives Resolution no. 11 of 1949 non-Muslim citizens were guaranteed fundamental rights on a par with Muslim citizens, the Islamicisation of Pakistan gathered pace in subsequent years. In the first constitution promulgated in 1956 the nation was given the title 'Islamic Republic of Pakistan'. Afzal Iqbal terms this a recognition of intent rather than a *de jure* description of the state.[6] However, this title was a portent of things to come. Article 57 sought the elimination of riba (usury) as early as possible. The office of President was reserved for Muslims only, though the Speaker of the National Assembly (who could act as the President in the absence or death of the President) could be a non-Muslim. The President was enjoined to appoint within one year a commission to bring all laws into conformity with Islamic principles. It is to be noted that the Christians had no representation in the Constituent Assembly that framed these stipulations.[7]

In the revised constitution of 1973 Islam is declared as the state religion of Pakistan (Para 1 part 2). Article 227 again stipulated that all laws should be in conformity with Islamic principles (other than the personal laws of non-Muslims, i.e. in matters such as marriage, divorce and inheritance). The position of Prime Minister was also reserved exclusively for Muslims in addition to that of President. These provisions are a blow to the equality that was envisaged by Jinnah and other founders of Pakistan. Religion is thus increasingly becoming the criteria, rather than citizenship and merit, by which people are judged and valued. No wonder that Mumtaz Ahmad adjudges that Islam has played a very important role in the constitutional debates in Pakistan.[8] In fact, Islam has been projected as the state ideology governing all aspects of public life in the country. In 1977 Prime Minister Bhutto, himself not a fundamentalist and supporting a secularist ideology, gave in to opposition demands and announced the introduction of Shari'a law and changed the weekly holiday from Sunday to Friday. Zia is said to have appropriated into the state the powers of religious institutions. Many Ulama became participants in policy-making and such higher echelons of the Zia administration without going through a democratic process. Thus the Islamic revivalism that took place under Zia was politicised and ideological not pietist.[9]

It is not as if the Christians of Pakistan had given any provocation for this discriminatory attitude by Muslims. They are not *ahl al Dhimma,* i.e. subject to the Muslims or the Muslim state by virtue of having been conquered. They just happened to be living in the Pakistan region when the subcontinent was partitioned in 1945. They saw no reason to emigrate to Hindu India. They are more of *ahl al Zulh*, people of a treaty, people who had become subject to the state of Pakistan by virtue of a treaty between the British and the state of Pakistan, without any intervention of their own. Alternatively they could be described as *ahl al Amn* (people who are safe) which is as they should be though the reality may be different. The Christians had

5   *Papers presented at the International Congress of Quaid I Azam* II (no date), p. 18.
6   Iqbal, Afzal, *Islamisation of Pakistan* (Delhi, 1984), p. 65.
7   See Fazl-ud-din, Joshua, *The Future of Christians in Pakistan* (Lahore, 1949), p. 10.
8   Ahmad, p. 102.
9   Ibid., p. 106.

also a role to play in the independence movement, though some have accused them of supporting the so-called 'Christian' British colonial regime. At the most, many of them may have stayed neutral. As Joshua Fazl-ud-din remarks, Christianity and national freedom had always gone hand in hand.[10] Christians seem to have adjusted well to the partition of India, both on the Indian as well as the Pakistani side. After independence they had completely thrown off the mantle of neutrality which some Christians had assumed during the independence struggle, and tried to be good citizens of the state in which they found themselves. Perhaps as Joshua Fazl-ud-din remarks they were following Christ's adage 'render to Caesar what belongs to Caesar and to God what belongs to God'[11] (Luke 20:25). As a matter of fact, the Christians had remained mainly passive in spite of the fact that those who were tenants of Hindu Zamindars who had emigrated to India sometimes faced eviction from their lands by their new Muslim masters. Moreover, Muslim refugees from India had in many a case displaced Christians in rural areas and created unemployment, for instance at harvest times.

Christians have from the beginning shown that they will be loyal to the state in which they found themselves. They are ready to give of their best to the state. However, if they are persistently denied equal opportunities and made subject to discrimination and hostility their enthusiasm will inevitably wane. They cannot be loyal to a state that defines nationhood and citizenship solely in terms of one religion and sees the rest as aliens. As Professor Kamal Faruqi notes, they would therefore be much happier if the ideal of the Islamic state is abandoned.[12] It is only human in such circumstances to feel less than wholly patriotic. But the Christians of Pakistan have never revealed themselves to be subversive of the state by word or deed. In a poll 92 per cent of Christians said that they are resolved to be a good Pakistani.[13] This in spite of the fact that even moderate Muslims often doubt their loyalty to the state of Pakistan.[14] Moreover, Christians in Pakistan are often looked down upon owing to their origins from the lower echelons of society such as the Chuhras (sweepers). The majority community in any case will tend to look upon them as inferior citizens such as the *ahl al dhimma*. Mawdudi, the great Islamic ideologue of the subcontinent had once said, 'The rights of non-Muslims in an Islamic state are those conferred on them by the Shari'a. The Islamic state is an ideological state not a national state. Non-Muslims cannot participate in policy-making, only in administration'.[15] No wonder some Christians made this sweeping statement about Pakistan, 'We are not Pakistanis. Every one belongs to a Biraderi, a tribe or a religious sect. This is because of our rulers' suppression and distortion of the political process'.[16] They might be particularly alluding to the formation of separate electorates by Zia but also referring

---

10 Fazl-ud-din, p. 29.
11 Fazl-ud-din, p. 39.
12 Quoted in Butler and Chagathai, p. 343.
13 Ibid., p. 346.
14 Ibid., p. 341.
15 Quoted in Butler and Chagathai, p. 338.
16 See Ghazzali, Abdul Sattar, *Islamic Pakistan, Illusions and Reality* (Islamabad, 1996), p. 239.

to the general alienation and discrimination by the majority community. Rai Shakil Akthar concurs. He states: 'A sense of community and nationhood has weakened over the years. Today Pakistan is divided on ethnic and sectarian lines'.[17] So Christians are not arguing for a separate autonomy or rights as a community but freedom to function as fully autonomous individuals in a liberal democratic nation with equal opportunities and with equal access to education, technology, employment etc.

But Pakistan is nowadays increasingly a state which is becoming communitarian rather than cherishing individual liberty and democracy, i.e. a community that is defined by Islam. The ethno-cultural-religious neutrality of the state is increasingly compromised, leading to difficulties for minority groups. I do not agree with Joshua Fazl-ud-din who opines that the relationship of Muslims and non-Muslims in Pakistan is that of the rulers and the ruled, nor with his recommendation that the best course for the latter is to fulfil duties as prescribed by laws pertaining to *ahl al dhimma* and not to clamour for their rights.[18] Geijebels tells us that a survey found that eighty per cent of Christians felt that they are second-class citizens.[19] But should they accept permanent marginalisation? This is far from the ideals of the founders of Pakistan. Will Kymlica suggests the possibility of creating their own economic, political and educational institutions.[20] This will be difficult in Pakistan where the majority is seeking to impose legal and political and even educational norms that are increasingly becoming defined by Islam. It should be remembered that once even Christian schools and colleges were nationalised, though now they have been given back to their Christian managements.

Violence against Christians and Christian institutions

This is increasingly a feature of Christian-Muslim relations in Pakistan. Pakistan is a hotbed of Islamist politics, augmented by the Afghan war on its borders, and the Kashmir issue against India, and the perennial victimisation of Palestinians by Israel. The Iraqi war has only heaped burning coals on fire. Therefore Pakistan has spawned a number of militant and extremist organisations. These Jehadi outfits have found a fertile ground in the obscurantist Madrassas and youths disillusioned by poverty, unemployment and corruption. The Muslim sections who are semi-literate and unenlightened have a narrow vision of world politics and will give tacit support to extremists. Violence against minorities, especially Christians, has therefore been on the increase, though the present government is strongly opposed to such illegal activities and will come down heavily on the perpetrators. But their measures have limitations and the enlightened Muslim majority are now mainly silent in the face of what they see as the American and Western crusade against Islam.

---

17 Akhtar, Rai Shakil, *Media, Religion and Politics in Pakistan* (Oxford, 2000), p. 222.

18 Fazl-ud-din, p. 58.

19 Geijebels, M., 'Pakistan, Islamisation and the Christian Community' in *Al-Mushir*, 22/3 (1980): 99-109, p. 100.

20 Kymlica, Will, *Politics in the Vernacular, Nationalism, Multiculturalism and Citizenship* (Oxford, 2001), p. 28.

I will not here discuss in detail the consequences of the Blasphemy Law since I have reserved a chapter exclusively for such discussion. The Blasphemy Law has increasingly become a tool for the persecution of Christians in Pakistan. It is ill-defined and liable to much abuse. The enforcers of law such as the police often collude with unjust accusations of blasphemy, and the judiciary while just and fair cannot always counter the accusations. Lawyers are averse to defending the accused since they can become the target of Muslim fanatics and extremists. Even a judge who acquitted a Christian accused of blasphemy has been assassinated. Christians who have been acquitted by the courts have been subject to extra judicial killings or social boycott and a climate of fear so that some have even left Pakistan for good, unable to countenance the stigma and oppression following blasphemy accusations.

Assaults on individual Christians or Christian homes are rare. Christian villages are an interesting phenomenon in Pakistan and point to some kind of ghettoisation of Christians in rural areas. Some of them such as Maryamabad have been brought about by utilisation of irrigated land made available by the Government of Pakistan and which had not been made use of by other communities.[21] The church had taken advantage of this and settled landless Christian labourers there to provide them with a means of livelihood. Bishop Malik, Moderator of the Church of Pakistan, also mentioned the existence of at least two dozen Christian villages. John Rooney mentions the instance of Christians being evicted from a village.[22] Malik Iftikhar talks of a 'massive uprooting' of the Christian population from Khanewal in March 1997 with the apparent blessings of the police.[23] As a matter of fact, right from the beginning, Joshua Fazl-ud-din states, minor officials had been harassing Christians in Pakistan and openly asking them to leave Pakistan, which they characterised as a homeland exclusively for Muslims.[24] This trend of mind, though not so openly expressed in recent times, might still be extant in the minds of some obscurantist and bigoted Muslim citizens. I put the question to Bishop Azariah whether Muslims of Pakistan are unhappy that there are non-Muslims in a state which is increasingly being defined as an Islamic State. He found this an interesting question and said that the Qur'an has a definite place for religions like Christianity, which is respected by them. But the problem is the history of Christian-Muslim relations and the fact that many Muslims associate the Christians with the colonial regime or the West and would feel uncomfortable with their presence in Pakistan.

But most of the violence has been against Christian institutions such as churches. I cite below some instances:

The Christian Voice of 8 February 2004 reports that gunmen disrupted the St Paul's church, Kasur, and fired three rounds and threatened to demolish the church. The church had a butcher shop in front so this might have led to some contention between the church and the shop-owner. Economic reasons are often involved in inter-religious conflict.

---

21 See Walbridge, Linda, *The Christians of Pakistan* (London, 2003), Ch. 2, for an account of the Canal Christian Colonies.

22 Rooney, John, *Into Desert Sands* (Rawalpindi, 1986), p. 99.

23 Malik, p. 141.

24 Fazl-ud-din, p. 68.

Pastor Mukhtar Masih of Assemblies of God was also shot dead. He was reported to have been keen on evangelism and had sometimes broadcast sermons on a loudspeaker. However, he had stopped doing so when Muslims objected to his public preaching. Similarly, a Christian Pastor, one George Masih, had also been shot dead apparently for singing Christian songs in public.[25]

On 8 December 1992 a mob of 5,000 men attacked the Sacred Heart Church in Kemani. The church actually ran a relief operation to aid poor fishermen living nearby, supplying them with medicines and other useful materials, and it is a pity that a church engaged in humanitarian work should have been targeted. *The Christian Voice* states that the church might have been mistaken for a Hindu temple, as it was the time when Muslims of the subcontinent were incensed at the destruction of the Babri Masjid in Ayodhya.[26] However temple and church architecture are vastly different and this misunderstanding is rather surprising.

Seven Christians had been killed in an attack on a Christian school in Murree. However, three of the assailants had been sentenced to death in a court of law.[27] *The Christian Voice* of 25 January 2004 reports a grenade attack on the Pakistan Bible Society buildings. An attack on the Holy Trinity Church of Karachi was condemned by both Christians and Muslims at a meeting organised by the NCIDE.[28] On Christmas Eve of 2002 sixteen worshippers at Christmas Sunday school celebrations at a church in Sianwaldi near Sialkot were killed when veiled militants hurled grenades at them. This was said to have been the work of the Jaish-I-Muhammad, a proscribed militant organisation. Apparently, prior to this a cleric in a local mosque had continually made hate speeches against Christians. This kind of fomenting of hatred against non-Muslims is unfortunately often a feature of mosque services in many places. Even mosques in the United Kingdom were not immune to this practice until the Muslim Council of Britain banned all political discussion in mosques, and the weekly *qutbah* (sermon) at the Jumah Namas on Fridays had to restrict itself to purely theological and spiritual themes. But the preachers in British mosques were no doubt inflamed by the participation of Britain in the Iraq war and aggrieved also by the persecution of fellow Muslims in Palestine by Israel, seemingly abetted by Britain and the United States. Whether the Muslim Kathibs (preachers) in Pakistan had any such viable motivation is difficult to ascertain. In the recent context the participation of Christian nations in the Iraq and Afghan wars may be a cause. However, hate against the innocent Christians of Pakistan is difficult to understand and such preaching against them hard to justify.

On 28 October 2001 five militant Muslims sprayed bullets on the congregation of the St Dominic Church in Bhawalpuri, killing 16 worshippers including 8 children.[29] On 17 March 2002 the Protestant International Church in Islamabad attended by a number of expatriates was attacked with grenades, killing five members of the

---

25 *The Christian Voice* (25 April 2004).
26 Ibid.
27 *The Christian Voice* (4 April 2004).
28 *The Christian Voice* (11 February 2004).
29 Rooney, John, *On Rocky Ground* (Rawalpindi, 1987), p. 156.

congregation.[30] The same year on 5 August masked extremists shot and killed six students in a Christian school of Murree.[31] On 25 September 2002 three terrorists attacked a human rights organisation, the Idara-e-Amin-o-Insaf, and killed seven human rights officials.[32] On 9 August 2003 four persons including three nurses were killed by grenade-throwing militants in the Christian Eye Hospital in Taxila.[33]

The attacks on Christian institutions have created a climate of fear among the Christian community. I found that The Christian Study Centre of Rawalpindi, noted for its dialogical work and for promoting harmony among Christians and Muslims, had no display board in front of the building, making it immensely difficult for a newcomer like me to find out its location. On reaching the institution I found that there was tight security there and an armed guard checked out my credentials thoroughly before letting me in, probably to ensure that I was not carrying any weapons or explosives. There is an armed guard in front of every church during worship times to protect the congregations from attack, though how effectively a lone soldier could defend the church against assailants is open to question. Bishop Malik told me that these guards were not posted on the Churches' request and was a governmental initiative. However, it points to the ever-present danger of a sudden attack by Muslim fanatics and militants.

The Iraq war and the alliance of the Musharaff administration with the United States in the war on terror seem to have worsened the hostility of Muslim fundamentalists against Christians. Archbishop Lawrence Saldhana of Lahore on a recent visit (June 2006) to the United States mentioned this fact and that aggression against Christians had been increasing in recent times. The Archbishop pointed out that while the Muslim masses were already adversely predisposed to Christians on account of their low social and economic status and their origins from the lower echelons of society, they have become quite unpopular with radical Muslims since the strategic alliance of Pakistan and the United States. The Archbishop cited the case of the incident in November 2005 when a mob of 3000 had destroyed three churches in Sangla near Lahore, and also attacked two Christian schools, a hostel and a convent after false allegations that some Christians had burned a copy of the Qur'an. The church had then formed district-level peace committees involving Christians and Muslims to calm the situation after such a traumatic event and to try to prevent recurrence of such incidents.

Problems in education

Educational institutions are a key factor in forming the attitudes of citizens. Therefore it is important that teachers and educational materials promote correct attitudes in young minds such as inter-religious harmony, tolerance, sensitivity to others, empathy, and avoidance of prejudice and bias. Unfortunately, the educational system in Pakistan is to some extent vitiated by religious bias and intolerance. This

---

30 Ibid.
31 Ibid.
32 Ibid.
33 Ibid.

is certainly a consequence of the escalating Islamicisation of the state that had its greatest momentum during the regime of Zia ul Haqq and which is very difficult to set right now. In the classical system of Islamic government the *Dhimmi* have to follow the educational system of the Islamic state. So the situation of Christians in Pakistan, at the least in this respect, resembles that of *ahl al Dhimma* in an Islamic state.[34]

The Justice and Peace Commission of the Roman Catholic Church of Pakistan has pointed out that syllabi are not based on democratic values and are discriminatory to non-Muslim students.[35] In my interviews with Bishops Malik and Azariah both have pointed out this difficulty with education in Pakistan. Bishop Malik emphasised that he has no objection to Christians studying Islam. As a matter of fact he encouraged Christian boys and girls to study Islam. This was both to promote an authentic understanding of the Islamic faith by Christians and thus create an attitude of tolerance, understanding and religious harmony and also so that they could score better marks. Students can offer Civics as an option to Islamic Studies, but then, Bishop Malik said, that the teachers, most of whom are Muslim, would recognise the candidate to be a non-Muslim and mark them down in examinations. This is certainly biased and unethical action, but this was life in Pakistan, the Bishop said. He also mentioned that a Muslim girl had once stood first in Christian scriptures in a Christian school. This reveals an exemplary attitude. *The Christian Voice* also points out that educational materials are insensitive to religious minorities.[36] Bishop Azariah stated that study of Islamiyyat is not the problem. But Islamicisation has filtered into even other subjects such as History, Civics and Social Studies. For instance, one textbook asks 'who are Pakistanis?' and gives the answer as 'Muslims'. Another states that Pakistan belongs to Muslims. So Islamiyyat spills over into other subjects – according to *The Christian Voice* even into the study of English and Urdu.[37] The journal also alleges that in some classes non-Muslims are compelled to memorise passages from the Qur'an and the rituals of *wudu* (ablutions preparatory to the prayer ritual) and also the prayer ritual itself. How much these are relevant to non-Muslims is not considered.[38] Bishop Azariah also said that the depiction of Christianity at higher-level classes is negative. Regarding the relationship of Christianity and Islam the only issues that are discussed are the Crusades and the colonial era, both not conducive to promotion of inter-faith harmony. No wonder if this is what is taught in educational institutions in Pakistan, as Iftikhar Malik writes: 'By reverting to a tunnel view of history in an aura of exaggeration, the age-old religious tensions between Christianity and Islam are frequently cited to substantiate alarmist hypotheses of a so-called clash of civilisations'.[39]

---

34 See Butler and Chagathai, p. 340.

35 *The Christian Voice* (25 July 2004).

36 *The Christian Voice* (11 April 2004).

37 Ibid.

38 Ibid.

39 Malik, Iftikhar H., *Islam, Nationalism and the West: Issues of Identity in Pakistan* (London, 1999), p. xvi.

The Christian Voice alleges that textbooks contain hate material about the Hindus.[40] Some texts apparently define Pakistan as a Muslim country with reference to India as a Hindu country. This depiction of religiously pluralistic nations is evidently erroneous and calculated to incite hatred of minorities and a neighbouring nation.

Bishop Malik is of the view that material about Christianity should either be written by Christian scholars or alternatively omitted altogether. Apparently, the Minister of Education has given the assurance that hate material will be taken out and non-Muslims prevented from studying matters that are not relevant to them.[41]

It has to be noted that Islamiyyat is a compulsory subject in competitive examinations leading to employment in the Central Superior Services and knowledge of Islam essential for admission to vocational and technical training institutions.[42] It is also included in all Police training institutions, though this is beneficial for police work in a Muslim majority state. These requirements will prove detrimental to the opportunities of non-Muslims in employment and training for employment.

General Zia's venture to bring education into line with the 'people's faith and ideology,' (no doubt meaning Islam) entailed the revision of curricula to organise the content around Islamic thought.[43] The idea was to foster deep loyalty to Islam and Muslim nationhood. This objective makes clear the bias and distortions of other faiths found in the curriculum. A similar revision of syllabi was attempted by the Bharathiya Janatha Party administration of India (1998-2004) in their venture to saffronise or Hinduise education but which met with stiff resistance by many impartial scholars and educators and the left-wing political parties. Zia's educational reforms also involved *inter alia* review of textbooks to expunge material repugnant to Islam. Segregation of the sexes in educational institutions was another feature of Zia's reforms. Muslims do not favour co-education, especially of older children.

Problems in the legal sphere

The law is the final source for redress of grievances, especially for minorities and such marginalised communities whose economic and political power are minimal. Thus in a democracy the courts of law and legislation should ensure the avoidance of laws that are prejudicial to the safety, standing and dignity of minorities. In many democracies the law often errs on the side of caution where minority matters are concerned. All organs of law, the legislators, the Police, judges and lawyers should ensure that the rights of minorities are protected as much as the rights of the majority community. Will Kymlica has proposed that minority human rights have to be determined not by a single international code but by the appropriate specific minority rights in each country. He also suggests that an international body has to

---

40 Ibid.

41 Ibid.

42 Iqbal, Afzal, *Islamisation of Pakistan* (Delhi, 1984), p. 118.

43 See Miner, Ahmad, 'Education', in Raza, Rafi (ed.), *Pakistan in Perspective 1947-1997* (Oxford, 2001), p. 247.

monitor the implementation and enforcement of these rights.[44] But such a move will meet with vehement opposition from the majority community in Pakistan where autonomy and sovereignty of the nation is held as sacrosanct.

The fact is that minority rights in law have been seriously compromised by the introduction of measures involving enforcement of the Shari'a during Zia ul Haqq's regime. As Mumtaz Ahmad states, Islam has played a very important role thereafter in the country's constitutional debates and political disputes. She states: 'Both in terms of rhetoric as well as policies Islam has been projected as the state ideology'.[45] The rights of non-Muslims in such an ideological state is that conferred by the Shari'a. The establishment of a Council of Islamic Ideology which does not have any non-Muslim representation is designed to bring all laws into conformity with the Shari'a.[46] The Enforcement of Shari'a act of 1991 has provided for the Islamicisation of the judicial system. The Federal Shari'a Court established by Zia in 1973 has jurisdiction over action in any other court and could review and revise such judgements. It could even set aside the enactments of Parliament.[47] All these could very well compromise the rights of religious minorities under law. Apparently the testimony of non-Muslims, like those of women, has been made secondary to that of Muslims. The judges presiding in the Shari'a court are all Muslim. The Shari'at Appellate Bench in the Supreme Court which has the power to review judgements of the Federal Shari'a Court also has no non-Muslim judges but could have two ulama as judges. The Islamic Penal Code has become a symbol of the Islamicisation of Pakistan.

The Supreme Court had given Zia the power to amend the constitution, a prerogative he duly exercised, and exempted martial law orders from judicial review with retrospective effect. This dealt a severe blow to the rule of law, and aided Zia in the Islamicisation process. He could also remove judges who were appointed by the previous Bhutto administration and those who were not amenable to the Martial Law Administrator.[48] The independence and integrity of judges were heavily compromised when Zia asked them to take an oath restricting their power of questioning the legitimacy of martial rule. Nineteen judges refused and were sacked. Zia even threatened the closure of the higher courts if his rival Bhutto was acquitted on his appeal to the Supreme Court regarding his rather dubious conviction for murder.[49] Thus Zia effectively removed the power of the judges to decide whether legislation was valid.[50] On 15 June 1988 in an ordinance Zia declared the Shari'a to be the supreme law of the land. Ulama now could be appointed as judges and challenge all existing laws of the nation. As a matter of fact Christians have demanded that cases involving Christian marriage and divorce issues should be heard by Christian judges,

---

44 Kymlica, Will, p. 84.

45 Mumtaz, p. 102.

46 *The Christian Voice*, 25 July 2004.

47 *Al-Mushir*, 45/4 (2003): 115.

48 See Malik, Hafeez, *Pakistan, Founders' Aspirations and Today's Realities* (Oxford, 2001), p. 71.

49 See Abbas, p. 95.

50 Ghazzali, Abdul Sattar, *Islamic Pakistan: Illusion and Reality* (Islamabad, 1996), p. 122.

but at present they are heard by City Government Nazims who have no legal training whatsoever.[51] On the other hand there are Muslims who say that a Christian judge cannot try a Muslim in court.[52]

Scholars have pointed to the politicisation and Islamicisation of judges. The independence and integrity of judges are heavily compromised if they and their families are under threat by the police and the secret service, or Islamist Jehadis. From the beginning itself the Islamicisation trend meant that judges were safer if they were conservative rather than liberal. They conformed more to *the taqleedi*[53] spirit of Islamic jurisprudence than to a liberal spirit.[54] In Pakistan judges are anyway subservient to the civil administration and the rulers. Moreover, they came to look upon the army as the real power in the state. During Zia's time the judges tended to project themselves as ulama. Zia appointed judges who were favourable to the Islamicisation of the state. These circumstances weighed heavily against the rights of minorities such as the Christians, a trend not wholly absent even now. Khaled Ahmed points out that the British principle of judges remaining aloof from the executive and legislators was abandoned, and judges called socially on influential political and bureaucratic figures in spite of the contingency that they might have to meet them in court and sit in judgement on cases involving them.[55]

The judiciary of Pakistan is thus seen to be pragmatic and politicised rather than impartial and principled. The judiciary had compromised with martial law administrations, deeming them justified on account of state necessity, though they were obviously unconstitutional. Thus in effect the constitution of the country has been compromised in the judicial process. The ultimate recourse for the redressal of grievances and upholding of minority rights is thus seen to be tainted and weak. No wonder Imran Khan in his interview told me that Pakistan does not have a strong and independent judicial system and every law is liable to be distorted and misused. His party is known as Tehreek Insaaf, The Justice Party, and no doubt he believes that reform of the legal sphere is critical to progress in Pakistan.

Problems in the religious domain

The Universal Islamic declaration of Human Rights to which Pakistan is a signatory states: 'The Qur'anic principle "There is no compulsion in religion" shall govern the religious rights of non-Muslim minorities' (Article X Section a). In addition it states: 'Every person has the right to freedom of conscience and worship in accordance with his religious beliefs' (Article XIII). The Pakistan Constitution of 1956 states: 'To God almighty belongs sovereignty over the whole universe and the authority delegated to the state of Pakistan through its people is to be exercised within the

---

51 See *Pakistan Christian* (2 February 2007).

52 Fazl-ud-din, p. 77.

53 Taqlid – In Islam this term means following an Islamic scholar with the ability to interpret the scriptures.

54 Ahmed, Khaled, *Pakistan, The State in Crisis* (Lahore, 2002), p. 265.

55 Ibid., p. 267.

limits prescribed by Him'. It continues: 'Adequate provision will be made for the minorities freely to profess and practise their religions and develop their cultures'.

The Objectives Resolution, which was in the preamble of the Constitution of 1956, states in paragraph G: 'Provision shall be made to safeguard the legitimate interests of the minorities'.

Though all these provisions for freedom of worship and professing of minority religions are there it is clear that, as Fazl-ud-din states, the legitimacy mentioned depends very much on Islamic principles and interests of the Muslims, so that these will not be rights but concessions granted by Islamic principles.[56] In Para B it is clearly stated, 'Wherein the principles of democracy, freedom, equality, tolerance and social justice as enunciated in Islam shall be fully observed'. The Objectives Resolution was in Zia Ul Haqq's time brought into the main body of the Constitution in Art 2A (annexure) and the word *freely* in the earlier quotation ominously omitted. It is also interesting, though you cannot always rely on reports from the United States about Islamic nations, that Pakistan was recommended by the US Commission on International Religious Freedom in May 2006 to be designated a 'Country of Particular Concern' by the Department of State 'because of the government's toleration of 'systematic, ongoing, and egregious violations of religious freedom'.[57]

Though individual Christians are not attacked, except in cases where blasphemy allegations have been made against them, as I have citied earlier in this chapter there are numerous incidents of attacks against churches. It is significant that often these attacks were made when worship was going on in the churches. This clearly indicates that the motivation for these assaults is religious, namely hostility against the Christian faith. These acts are obviously intended to intimidate Christians into not professing their religion openly. There is no prohibition against propagating one's faith but attacks against evangelists clearly show that propagation of Christianity among Muslims is taboo and will be met with severe reprisals.

The rise of Wahabist ideology in Pakistan as all over the Islamic world may be a factor in this hostility to the practice and profession of Christianity. Wahabism is rigorous and puritanical and will not countenance any absorption of ideas and practices from other faiths. The main agency for the spread of Islam in the Indian Subcontinent was Sufism, not a strait-laced form of Islam such as Wahabism, though now with the oil wealth of Saudi Arabia, the headquarters of Wahabism, the ideology has been able to make much headway all over the world. But Islam's agency in the Indian Subcontinent was the mystical, contemplative and spiritual form that is enshrined in the practice of Sufism. Sufis found much affinity with religious figures of other faiths. As a matter of fact Sufism was to allow many practices which strictly speaking are only possible in other faiths. It is noteworthy that the Shirdi Sai Baba of Ahmednagar in India, while a Muslim, is also highly revered by Hindus even now. This flexibility of Sufism meant that for many Hindus conversion in earlier times to Islam was not the disruptive factor for their lives or culture that it is now. Butler and Chagathai state that many Sufis of Pakistan are sympathetic to Christianity and

---

56 Fazl-ud-din, p. 87.
57 Reported in *Today's Christian* (January-February 2007).

consider Catholic priests as their counterparts in Christianity.[58] But Wahabism is very Arab-oriented and not very amenable to cultural osmosis or even adaptation. It can be seen that Wahabism is unlikely to promote much toleration of other faiths or inter-religious dialogue. The Taliban was one of the foremost proponents of Wahabi ideology in the world and their destruction of the Bamiyan Buddhas, a world heritage, is symptomatic of their intolerance of other faiths. It is true that there are Christian groups who have a similar ideology *vis-à-vis* Islam or other non-Christian faiths. Many of them are seen in the southern Untied States. But there have been no complains of their treatment of religious minorities in the USA. As for the Christian community of Pakistan, they are seen to be actively promoting inter-religious dialogue especially with Islam.

The association of Islam and the state is clearly spelt out in the 1973 constitution, which avers that Islam is the state religion of Pakistan. The secular ideals of the founders of Pakistan have therefore foundered on the rock of Islamicisation. Mrs Imtiaz, a teacher in a Christian school and a Christian activist, was very informative on the status of Christians in Pakistan. Regarding freedom of worship, Mrs Imtiaz admitted that Christians also could celebrate their festivals and hold public meetings. They have also the liberty to process. But these are mostly held in the church premises. Not that there is any legal prohibition against holding it in other venues, but discretion enjoins Christians not to hold public events away from the churches. Mrs Imtiaz said that the Muslims of Pakistan 'are not of that mind', probably implying that such incursions will not be looked upon favourably and might invite reaction of an extreme nature. Christian conventions are held mainly for Christians, though Muslims are not prohibited from attending. But they are not invited openly for the same reasons as why most Christian celebrations are held at Church venues. No Christian radio or television programmes exist, but Christian movies are available on Cable Television. Foreign stations broadcasting Christian programmes such as the FEBA (Far East Broadcasting Association) can be heard. Selling or playing Christian CDs in public is not advisable. Mrs Imtiaz said that the present government is protective and supportive, but the Muslim masses 'over the years have been brain-washed and given a mentality to abhor anything that is not Islam'. Strong words indeed!

On the other hand, there are misgivings about the incorrect and pejorative portrayal of Christians in TV, Radio and Films. Butler and Chagathai propose a committee to look into the portrayal of Christianity and Christians in the media and advise the Government.[59] *The Christian Voice* also reports that State-owned Pakistan Television broadcasts serials depicting Mohammad bin Kasim, Shaheen and Tippu Sultan which are obvious misrepresentations of history and disadvantageous to non-Muslims.[60]

Bishop Malik agrees that there is freedom to practise Christianity. Conventions are also able to be arranged, and nobody bothers or disrupts such meetings. For processions such as a Bible Walk permission has to be sought, presumably from

---

58 Butler and Chagathai, p. 333.

59 Ibid., p. 345.

60 *The Christian Voice* (25 July 2004).

the Police or the District Commissioner. Bishop Malik, however, commented that the Churches have problems in celebrating the Eucharistic ritual. Since alcohol is *haram* (forbidden) in Islam there is no sale of liquor in Pakistan. It is difficult therefore to procure wine needed for the Holy Communion sacrament. Bishop Malik considers this an infringement of freedom of religion, though I take this view as an exaggeration. However, it will be necessary to note that in classical Islam non-Muslims are allowed to use wine and even sell wine, provided that they do not become inebriated.[61]

The constitutional provision for freely professing and practising religion perhaps implies the propagation of one's faith as part of the profession of religion. Both Islam and Christianity are keen proselytising faiths and the dawa'h organisations in Pakistan such as the Jamat ud Dawa'h are not behind anyone in trying to gain adherents to Islam. *The Christian Voice* of 16 May 2004 reports that, during the years 1999 to 2003, 646 non-Muslims converted to Islam. Bishop Malik is of the opinion that not many Christians are lost by conversion to Islam. A few are pragmatic and will convert in order to obtain easy divorce. Divorce laws in Islam are not as convoluted and procedurally arduous as in the Christian case. Usually the male has the prerogative of divorcing a wife by the triple pronouncement of the word *talaq* (I divorce you). The Christian divorce laws of Pakistan, according to Bishop Malik, were framed in 1872 and allow divorce only on grounds of adultery – somewhat in line with Christ's injunctions.[62] However, the accusation of adultery would invite the application of the draconian Hudood Laws against adultery. I have already mentioned that there are cases where Christian girls are kidnapped and forcibly converted to Islam, but in general forcible conversions to Islam are rare.

It is to be noted as I stated earlier that in the provision for freedom to profess and practise religion by religious minorities the word 'freely' was omitted by Zia in the 1973 constitution. This indicates that the constitution will disapprove of the propagation of minority religions in Pakistan, particularly among Muslims. Even otherwise, Christian proselytisation of Muslims is almost impossible. Though the law of apostasy does not operate in Pakistan and conversion from Islam to other faiths is legally permissible, the convert runs considerable risk of being assassinated by extremists. Butler and Chagathai mention the case of a Christian missionary running a correspondence course in Christianity which has apparently recruited six thousand subscribers.[63] Some of the Muslims enrolled have been converted to Christianity. But conversion from Islam to Christianity is exceptional in Pakistan. Mrs Imtiaz admits that there are many evangelistic organisations. These carry out, in the words of Mrs Imtiaz, 'muffled' evangelisation – i.e. not open, but confidential and person to person – and carried out on an individual basis through private conversations, and in her words at 'a controlled pace'.

Peace World Wide, an NGO connected to the United Nations, mentions the case of two young Christians who tried to distribute Christian tracts in Jacobabad.

---

61 See Doi, Rahman A, *Non-Muslims Under Shari'ah* (Lahore, 1981), pp. 53-4.

62 Matthew 5:32: 'But I say unto you, that whosoever shall put away his wife, saving for the cause of fornication, causeth her to commit adultery'.

63 Butler and Chagathai, p. 330.

The young men were arrested and badly beaten by the police in the police station. The ulama there apparently escalated the issue into a campaign against the entire Christian community.[64] Shots were fired at Christ Church, Jacobabad, and the office of the pastor of the church broken into. The pastor has also received death threats. The young men were ill advised in their action, but since these acts were not illegal it is not clear on what grounds they were arrested. This is another instance of how elements of the judicial machinery such as the police occasionally tend to be swayed by popular sentiments and ignore the stipulations of the law.

It is clear that while there is freedom to practise Christianity in Pakistan with certain restrictions, the constitutional provisions are heavily weighed against equal rights for religious minorities. This is due to the increasing Islamicisation of the constitution and the governmental system. The judiciary, the bureaucracy and the legislature are heavily oriented towards this. No wonder that Justice Cornelius once remarked 'I am a constitutional Muslim'.[65] Even otherwise, as Linda Walbridge comments, there is an overt influence of Islamic ethos on the practice of Christianity in Pakistan.[66] Pakistan churches are also making a conscious effort to indigenise the practice of Christianity in Pakistan – in the liturgy, in church music and rituals. Arabic names are popular among Christians – this is obviously to remove the trappings of Western culture from Christianity, which in the main was brought to Pakistan by missionaries from the West with Western cultural characteristics. This is not due to coercion by Muslims but is intended to improve inter-religious relations and to prove that Christianity is as much of an indigenous religion in Pakistan as Islam. As a matter of fact the advent of Christianity into Pakistan preceded that of Islam as I have discussed in Chapter 2. However, there are problems in education, in meting out justice and in the profession of Christianity. Even in classical Islam the *ahl al dhimma* were not barred from propagating their religions. The freedom and impartiality and fairness implied in the constitution are not to be found nowadays and are steadily compromised by implementation of laws such as the Blasphemy Law.

President Musharaff has exhorted Muslims to follow a policy of enlightened moderation.[67] He advocates that Muslims shun militancy and extremism and adopt the path of socio-economic uplift. He calls upon the West to resolutely resolve all political injustices (probably he is referring to the Palestinian issue) and assist by uplifting the Muslim world socio-economically.[68] Political injustice and socio-economic deprivation might be at the heart of much Islamic extremism in the modern world. Anyway, it keeps the enlightened and moderate Muslim sections silent and strengthens the hands of the radicals and extremists. The present political climate of Pakistan and the Muslim world is hardly conducive to strengthening the hands

---

64 See *Peace World Wide* http://www.pww.org.pk/index.php?link=NewsDetails&mod=News&id=14&page=4.

65 Quoted in Butler and Chagathai, p. 349.

66 See Walbridge, L., Chapter 14, *An Islamic Christianity.*

67 Musharaff, Pervez, 'Time for enlightened moderation', in *Dawa'h Highlights*, XV/5 (May-June 2004): 5-8.

68 Ibid., p. 6.

of Muslim intellectuals and moderates. In general, uninformed Muslims can easily be swayed by the arguments of the militants for joining fundamentalist and jehadi movements.

Christians in Pakistan think of themselves as Pakistanis, full-fledged citizens of the state sharing the aspirations, problems and vicissitudes of history with Muslims and other citizens of the country. The dilemma for them is how to reconcile this vision with the increasing Islamicisation of the nation, the coalescence of national identity with Islam and the discrimination on many fronts that they are subject to. It will need a sea-change in the attitude of the Muslims of Pakistan and a reversal of the escalating policy of Islamicisation of the state to achieve this.

Chapter Five

The Blasphemy Law and its impact on the Christian community

The classical definition of blasphemy involves disparaging remarks about God, but in common parlance in the West blasphemy has come to mean any indifferent or irreverent act, words or attitude to anything that is generally considered sacrosanct or inviolable. In European and American law blasphemy concerns such acts, sayings or attitudes which violate the sanctity of God, or the other members of the Holy Trinity. Blasphemy could also occur if one claimed to be God or possess powers similar to God. Indeed the first Sufi martyr, Mansur al Hallaj, was executed in 922 CE by the then Caliph for claiming to be God. His famous statement '*ana al Haqq*' (I am the Truth or God) was alleged to have threatened the security of the state due to his theological adventurism. Penalties for this offence in modern times come to a maximum of one year's imprisonment or a maximum fine of approximately $300. But Pakistan has one of the harshest of blasphemy laws, inviting draconian punishments such as life-long incarceration and even death. However, it is strange that the Blasphemy Law of Pakistan does not have specific reference to disparaging the name of Allah as it has to Prophet Muhammad and the Holy Qur'an, though it might be covered under general terms in some of its clauses.

The Blasphemy Law in the Pakistan Penal Code and Criminal Procedure Code is a significant factor in Christian-Muslim relations in Pakistan. The Blasphemy Law has been there in British India before the creation of Pakistan. The Indian Penal Code formulated in the 1860s by Lord Macaulay contained a clause (section 295) prohibiting the defiling of sacred places with the intention of wounding the religious sensibilities of different communities. The British were cognisant of the rivalry between different communities, probably exacerbated by their policy of *divide et impera*[1] and therefore they deemed such a law necessary to keep the peace between the various religious communities in the pluralistic Indian population. The clause reads:

> Whoever destroys, damages or defiles any place of worship, or any object held sacred by any class of persons with the intention of thereby insulting the religion of any class of persons or with the knowledge that any class of persons is likely to consider such destruction, damage or defilement as an insult to their religion, shall be punished with imprisonment of either description for a term which may extend to two years, or with fine, or with both.

---

1   Divide and rule.

In 1927 after the famous *Rangila Rasul* (The Jolly Prophet) case the law was expanded to include verbal and pictorial insults as well.

> Whoever, with deliberate and malicious intention of outraging the religious feelings of any class of citizens, by words, either spoken or written, or by visible representations insults the religion or the religious beliefs of that class, shall be punished with imprisonment of either description for a term which may extend to two years, or with fine, or with both.[2]

Rangila Rasul (The Jolly Prophet) was a scurrilous article on Prophet Muhammad written by Pandit Chamupati, a member of the Arya Samaj and published by Mahase Rajpal, that led to a famous trial in which the case was dismissed by a Sikh judge (probably since the law then did not include verbal defamation of religions). Rajpal himself was later assassinated by a Muslim. Consequently, Hindu-Muslim conflict ensued and several persons were killed. The British later added Sec 296 regarding disturbing a religious assembly and Sec 297 on trespassing on burial grounds.

However, the issue of the Blasphemy Law in Pakistan came to the limelight during the martial regime of General Zia ul Haqq (1977-1988). In 1985 he added clauses 295 B and 295 C which *inter alia* stipulated the death penalty for defaming the Prophet. Article 295 as mentioned above deals with injuring or defiling a place of worship with the intention of wounding religious sensibilities of any faith. The penalty prescribed is two years in prison or fine or both. Article 295A pertains to deliberate and malicious acts intended to outrage religious feelings of any group by insulting its religion or religious beliefs. The punishment is ten years in prison or fine or both. Article 295B relates to defiling of a copy of the Holy Qur'an. The penalty is life imprisonment. Finally, the most controversial of the laws – 295 C – relates to derogatory remarks in respect of Prophet Muhammad. This offence entails capital punishment or life imprisonment. In 1990 the religious parties took the matter to the Federal Shar'ia Court, stating that there should be a mandatory death sentence for this offence, and the Sharia court acquiesced. Thus the alternative life imprisonment clause was deleted from 295 C.[3] In 1992 both the National Assembly and Senate of Pakistan passed resolutions affirming this amendment to the Blasphemy Law.

The Blasphemy Law targets not only Christians, against whom the majority of cases have been brought, but also minority Islamic sects. The Ahamadiyya are a Muslim sect considered to be extremely heretical by Orthodox Muslims, and therefore there are provisions in the Blasphemy Law that relate to them specifically. In addition to the earlier provisions more elaborate regulations were also put in place by General Zia that include questioning of the finality of Prophet Muhammad who is perceived in orthodox Islam as the seal (*khatm*) of the prophets. This is no doubt a challenge to the Ahamadiyya who believe that the institution of prophets by God carried on after Prophet Muhammad and consider Mirza Ghulam Ahmad, the

---

2   By the Second Amendment, Act XVI of 1991, the term of imprisonment was extended to ten years in India.

3   Ghazi, Muhammad A., 'The Law of Tawhin-I-Risalat: A social, political and historical perspective', in Tarik Jan (ed.) *Pakistan between Secularism and Islam: Ideology, Power and Conflict* (Islamabad, 1998), pp. 209-40, p. 220.

founder of the sect, as the Prophet of the twentieth century. Other regulations that affect the Ahamadiyya specifically are as follows:

298 B relates to their considering Ahamad as the *Amir ul Mumineen* (Leader of the Faithful), a term which in classical Islam is reserved only for the Khalifa (Caliphs) of Islam. Similarly, use of *Ummul Mumineen* (Mother of the Faithful) for persons other than the wives of the Prophet (probably the Ahamadiyya referred thus to the wife of Mirza Ghulam Ahmad), *Ahl e Bait* (Family of the Prophet) presumably used by Ahamadiyyas to denote also the family of their founder, calling their place of worship *Masjid* and use of the word *Adhan* for their call to prayer.

It can be seen that these regulations are highly discriminatory and derogatory to the Ahamadiyya who consider themselves as Muslims, a status now denied officially to them in Pakistan.

Iftikhar Malik opines that General Zia carried out these amendments to the Blasphemy Law to appease orthodox Muslim elements in Pakistan.[4] This was evidently part of the Islamicisation of Pakistan that General Zia tried to effect, probably to strengthen the legitimacy of and garner popular support for his essentially unconstitutional regime.

There have been constant demands for the scrapping of the Blasphemy Law both from minorities in Pakistan as well as from abroad. The attitude of rulers of Pakistan succeeding General Zia to this demand has been ambiguous. President Musharaff himself has exhorted Muslims to shun the paths of militancy and extremism and is generally perceived to be moderate, fair and sympathetic to the minorities.[5] But he has recently categorically rejected an appeal by Amnesty International and the Justice and Peace Commission of the Vatican, which had written to the President requesting repeal of this law.[6]

People continue to be arrested under the Blasphemy Law. One of the most recent cases (24 May 2006) is that of Qamar David, a Christian who was arrested for sending blasphemous messages to Muslims on his cell phone, a modern turn on the issue. Shahbaz Bhatti, the Chairperson of the All Pakistan Minorities' Alliance called on the police to publish the content of the messages, which they refused to do. Mr Bhatti stated that he was apprehensive that Qamar David might be tortured in the police station and he and his family attacked by extremists and requested the police authorities to give them police protection.[7]

For one of the significant problems is that even if a person is acquitted of these charges he/she might be assassinated by fanatical vigilantes. Numerous such cases have happened. The case of Manzur, Rahmat and Salamat, a Christian family of Gujranwala, accused of blasphemy, is an instance. They were convicted and sentenced to death in the sessions court, allegedly for throwing scurrilous messages into a mosque, a verdict that was appealed and countermanded in the Lahore High

---

4 Malik, Iftikhar H., *Islam, Nationalism and the West: Issues of identity in Pakistan* (London, 1999), p. 303.

5 Musharaff, Pervez, 'Time for enlightened moderation', in *Dawah Highlights*, XV/5 (May-June 2004): 5-8, 6.

6 Reported in *The Peninsula* (Qatar Daily), (13 May 2006).

7 *AsiaNews* (30 May 2006).

court. As the accused were leaving the court they were all shot at and Manzur killed, according to Amnesty International, by members of the militant organisation Sipahi–I-Sahaba (Army of the Companions of the Prophet).[8]

Instances also abound when Christians accused of blasphemy have been tortured and in some instances killed by the police. It is extremely reprehensible when the guardians of the law themselves break the law. Standards of policing in the subcontinent are different from those of the West. Often the third degree is applied for obtaining evidence and confessions. Material obtained in this way is not reliable, and there are instances when the accused have succumbed to the rather brutal methods of their interlocutors. In the case of questioning under the Blasphemy Law such interlocution can be even more traumatic since most of the police staff are Muslims and will be emotionally involved in cases of affront to their religion. Samuel Masih, accused of blasphemy, died in police custody, killed by the policeman, one Faryad Ali, who was supposed to be guarding him.[9] Samuel Masih, who was a sweeper, was accused of throwing garbage on a stone plaque on which Qur'anic verses are inscribed. Most probably the sweeper was unaware of the offence that he had caused and his action had been an accident rather than an act of deliberate insult or provocation. One Tahir Iqbal was said to be poisoned to death in jail.[10] Apparently the jail warden had commented that people like him deserved to die. Ayyoub Masih, found guilty of blasphemy, was shot at while being escorted through the corridors of the sessions court of Sahiwal. The police took no action to apprehend the assailants.[11] Often confessions are obtained under torture and the value of confessions obtained under duress is manifestly dubious.[12]

An acquittal is thus no guarantee of immunity against violence for the accused in Blasphemy Law trials. As a matter of fact it is said that the law is frequently abused to settle personal scores or to put down an economic rival, dispossess a person from land and such personal and secular reasons rather than for genuine blasphemy against Islam. In some cases people are accused for reasons that are not specified in the statutes. Ayyoub Masih for instance was charged for allegedly speaking approvingly of Salman Rushdie's *The Satanic Verses*. In a way since the book is defamatory of the Prophet and his wives, approving it can be tantamount to defamation of the Prophet. But this is a rather contrived application of the law. Ayyoub has denied the accusations. Tahir Iqbal was charged with blasphemy for converting from Islam to Christianity. This should normally fall under the matter of apostasy, not blasphemy, but nevertheless he was charged under the Blasphemy Law and sentenced to death. In Pakistan there is no death penalty for apostasy, though in some Islamic states this is an offence that attracts the highest penalty. Baba Bantu, an elderly man, was

---

8   Walbridge, Linda, *The Christians of Pakistan, The Passion of Bishop Joseph* (London, 2003), p. 93.

9   *The Christian Voice* (6 June 2004): 7.

10 Ibid.

11 Walbridge, p. 90.

12 See the statement by Shabhaz Bhatti, Chairman of the All Pakistan Minorities Alliance (APMA), regarding obtaining confessions under torture in police custody, *AsiaNews.It* (29 May 2006).

apparently charged under the Blasphemy Law for possessing healing powers. How this can be construed as blasphemy is not clear. It may be indicative of Wahabi influence since the Wahabis are well known to be against Sufism, and charismatic and wonder-working individuals are related to Sufism. It might also be remembered that Sayyid Ahmad Khan, an influential ideologue from pre-partition India, was opposed to miracles and healing and such contra-natural activities. He construed these to be against the laws that God had instituted in the universe and therefore to be actions that work against God.[13] Islamic resurgence in many Sunni nations, such as Pakistan, Afghanistan, Malaysia or Indonesia is often seen to be influenced by such Wahabi ideals.

Lawyers are reluctant to defend the accused in Blasphemy Law cases, since violence may be directed against them as well as the accused in such cases. This poses a great problem for due process under law. Often the accused are poor and may not be able to afford to engage a lawyer. In such cases the government has to appoint a counsel or the government pleader for arguing their case. But it is difficult to find lawyers who are prepared to defend those accused of blasphemy. There was even an instance of a judge who acquitted a Christian family accused of blasphemy being assassinated. Judge Arif Iqbal Husain Bhatti who had acquitted Rahmat, Manzur and Anwar Masih mentioned earlier was shot and killed in October 1977.[14] It is an utter travesty of the legal process if vigilante action goes on unhindered to such an extent that even the judiciary are not safe.

Often these charges are brought nefariously to serve personal purposes. Malik Ifthikar states that frequently the motivation is to grab property belonging to Christians.[15] *The Times* reports that charges were fabricated against 15 Christians in 1998 to force them to drop a land dispute litigation.[16] It is true that even if Christians are acquitted they can no longer safely live in Pakistan. According to *The Christian Voice* there are instances of Christians being spirited out of the country for their own safety.[17] Linda Walbridge cites the case of Gul Masih, acquitted of charges of blasphemy, who was sent to Germany by Bishop John Joseph for his safety and was thereafter never reunited with his family in Pakistan.[18] This is a tragic instance of forced exile of an innocent man compelled to leave his country and his family. Asif Masih and Amjad Masih, two Christians from Jhang District, were arrested in 1999, falsely accused by the police of burning the Qur'an and sentenced to life imprisonment. The two have denied the accusations, stating that this was a trumped up charge brought by corrupt police officers when they refused to pay bribes to them. Their appeal to the High Court was rejected but the sentence was overturned in 2005 by the Supreme Court.[19] So for upwards of five years they were incarcerated

---

13 See Malik, Hafeez, *Sir Sayyid Ahmad Khan and Muslim Modernization in India and Pakistan* (New York, 1980), pp. 273-9.

14 Walbridge, p. 95.

15 Malik, Ifthikar, p. 303.

16 *The Times* (11 May 1998).

17 *The Christian Voice* (20 June 2004).

18 Walbridge, pp. 91-2.

19 *The Indian Catholic* (21 June 2006).

while awaiting the decision of the appellate courts, since desecrating the Qur'an is a non-bailable offence. Now the two are reported to be staying at secret locations for fear of extremists who have threatened to kill them.[20] Moreover the accused and their families would find it almost impossible to gain employment with Muslims. Christians in Pakistan are far from affluent, and are a struggling community. Their origins are mostly from the lowest echelons of society such as the Chuhras (sweepers). The blasphemy accusations compound their difficulties by denying them avenues for earning their livelihood. Amjad's wife, for instance, was working as a maid in a Muslim home but was sacked as soon as her employers heard about her husband being accused of blasphemy. She and her four children are being supported by a Christian organisation, but their life has become very difficult and almost unviable in Pakistan.

That most of the charges under the Blasphemy law are spurious is clear from the fact that most convictions by the lower courts have not been upheld by the appellate courts. This, in spite of the fact that the judges hearing these cases are Muslim. This says something about the integrity of the judicial system in Pakistan. But for the instituting of Shari'a courts by General Zia the system mainly follows the British system of justice. However, there is no jury trial in the subcontinent. A colonial government could not afford to do that as some of the litigation brought would have implications for the legitimacy of the judges and the court itself in colonial times, and matters relating to sedition and struggle for independence could very well have been thrown out by an Indian jury. It is strange that Independence from colonial rule has not brought about any change in this circumstance. However, in place of juries an appellate bench of two or more judges carry out this function. The system works fairly well, in spite of the fact that there is no popular representation in the justice system.

In some cases the reason for bringing a charge is merely gossip or rumour and will not stand up in court. An amendment to the laws was sought to be brought in 1995, whereby it becomes an offence to bring in false accusations of blasphemy, punishable with ten years' imprisonment. Moreover, the authorities were to investigate as to the *bona fides* of an accusation before registering a case under the Blasphemy Law. An official of no less standing than a Deputy Commissioner has to conduct the investigation. This would have been a salutary development since then no one would have brought accusations lightly. This amendment met resistance from the religious right and the Panjab and Balochistan assemblies passed resolutions against this amendment.[21] Even ministers have sometimes criticised the amendments. Minister for Religious Affairs Ijazul Haqq stated 'that the people of Pakistan would come out on the streets if attempts were made to change the Blasphemy Law'.[22] Elsewhere he stated that the law of the jungle would prevail if these statutes were ever abrogated.[23]

---

20 *The Telegraph* (25 June 2006).

21 Ghazzali, Abdul Sattar, *Islamic Pakistan: Illusions and Reality* (Islamabad, 1996), p. 237.

22 *Friday Times* (3-9 September 2004): 15.

23 *The Times* (11 May 1998).

Most recently he has stated vehemently that even if 100,0000 Christians lost their lives under the Blasphemy Law it will not be repealed.[24]

Christian organisations have also criticised the amendments but on the grounds that they do not go far enough. The Justice and Peace Commission of the Catholic Bishops' Conference objected on the grounds that the inhuman character of the law does not change under these amendments. It also alleges that Deputy Commissioners who are supposed to conduct a preliminary investigation of the *bona fides* of allegations under the Blasphemy Law, and even judges, are under pressure not to acquit the accused. Lawyers too, they said, are reluctant to defend them.[25] The amendments also do not address the issue of extra-judicial killings related to Blasphemy Law.

Therefore the clause regarding punishment for false accusations have been dropped though approved by the Federal Cabinet, but changes were made to procedure so that the FIR (First Information Report) cannot be filed without a magistrate first investigating as to the credibility of the accusations. In actual fact these measures have not been properly implemented due to paucity of time for the magistrates and more sinisterly since they are under pressure not to do so from extremists.[26] The Sub-Editor of *The Dawn* whom I interviewed confirmed that this amendment is often ignored and the police simply register cases. According to him the culture of investigating these accusations have to develop over the course of time. But for a law where the punishments are draconian and the consequences to the accused dire, accusations should not be allowed to be brought lightly. It is not a matter of a culture developing, such as tolerance of other faiths, but the strict interpretation and implementation of the law.

Imran Khan, the articulate, intelligent and charismatic opposition leader and chair of the Tareekh Insaaf (Justice Party), told me that the Blasphemy Law is well intentioned but not properly formulated. He called the Hudood and Blasphemy Laws half-baked. The intention of the Blasphemy Law is that, he said, that when different religious groups live together one should not insult another's religion. He pointed out that there is a blasphemy law in England also. But these laws are being misused in Pakistan to discriminate against women and the religious minorities. He stressed that there is a need to put a stop to this. He was of the opinion that in Pakistan not only these laws but every law is being misused. According to him there is no justice system in Pakistan. The judiciary are not strong enough – there is no law enforcement. The strong can get away with misusing any law to oppress the weak. Every law in Pakistan is distorted and misused, he said, because we do not have a strong and independent judiciary. In his opinion the Blasphemy and Hudood laws needed to be looked into again.

The fervour and even paranoia in some Muslim circles about enforcing the Blasphemy Law and accusing all and sundry under it, apart from occasions when it is misused for personal vendetta or economic gain, might be indicative of the general disturbed atmosphere of Pakistan. Apart from political instability manifested by the

---

24 *BosNews Life* (27 June 2006).
25 *The Christian Voice* (22 August 2004).
26 See *The Christian Voice* (22 August 2004).

many *coups d'état* and such unconstitutional developments in governance, Pakistan has been caught up in many controversies including wars and violence. The obvious instance is its perennial confrontation with India, mostly over the issue of Kashmir. Latterly it has been the traumatic political developments in Afghanistan, its other immediate neighbour. Since the Marxist coup of 1978 and the ensuing domination by the Soviet Union, the stormy history of Afghanistan has had severe repercussions on political stability in Pakistan as well. The internecine war after the departure of the Soviets has seen Pakistani regimes on the side of the Taliban. But the invasion of Afghanistan and the ouster of the Taliban regime by the USA has found Pakistan in a dilemma. Pakistan has always posed as the ally of the West in general and the USA in particular, *vis-à-vis* India, and therefore had to support the US in its new role in Afghanistan. But the collaboration of Pakistan with the United States against Islamic fundamentalists has not been approved by many Pakistanis, notably the Muslim Right. The Musharaff regime has therefore come in for considerable flak from extremists and hardliners in Islamic organisations in Pakistan and has had to tread carefully between its support of the West and condemnation of US intervention in the region. The quest to apprehend Osama bin Laden, now popularly believed to be in hiding somewhere in Pakistan, the fighting in Waziristan between the Taliban and its Pakistani sympathisers against the Pakistani army, and popular antipathy to the United States have thrown Pakistan into turmoil, and the Musharaff regime into instability. The subsequent Iraq war has only exacerbated the difficulties. The hostility against the West has vitiated to some extent the relations between Pakistani Muslims and the indigenous Christian community. The statement of Lawrence Saldhana, Catholic Archbishop of Lahore, that the wars in Afghanistan and Iraq have increased discrimination against Christians is significant in this context.[27] The Blasphemy Law has become a convenient tool for expressing hostility against Christians, who are erroneously perceived to be the allies of the USA and the West. Christian leaders have always hotly denied these allegations.[28] It has to be noted that though the Blasphemy Law was initially instituted in 1927 by the British the incidence of accusations under the Law have burgeoned in recent times. For instance, from 1927 to 1986 only 7 cases had been registered but since 1986 over 4000 accusations have taken place.[29] This can only reflect the growing turbulence and instability in Pakistan towards the latter part of the twentieth century.

A serious deficiency in the Blasphemy Law as it stands is that it relates to the religious sensibilities of the Muslims alone. In a multi-religious nation such as Pakistan the law should have provisions for scurrilous speech, writing and actions against the religiously revered elements in other faiths such as Christianity, Hinduism and Sikhism, religions which are minority faiths but nevertheless present in some number in Pakistan. These offences may be relating to their founders, scriptures, or places of worship. This is an anomaly which has given rise to the feeling that only the religious sensibilities of Muslims are sacrosanct in Pakistan. This is bound to make Pakistan a very sectarian society and in complete contradiction to the aspirations

---

27 *The Christian Voice* (11 July 2004).

28 For instance Bishop Andrew Francis. See *The Christian Voice* (1 February 2004).

29 *The Christian Voice* (25 July 2004).

and principles of its founders. The original legislation by the British had been set in more general terms and covered insults to all religions, not to any particular religion alone. In a democracy which is based on egalitarianism only such a law would be in conformity with fundamental rights and be respected by all. No wonder I.A. Rahim, recipient of the Magsaysay award of 2004 for peace and international understanding, states, 'These laws are retrogressive, because they discriminate against minorities, impinge on their rights to freedom of belief and pose a serious threat to their right to liberty. So these laws are in conflict with their constitutional and fundamental rights'.[30] He goes on to point out that these laws were instituted by Zia ul Haqq without the people's mandate.[31] The law has undoubtedly aggravated Muslim religious extremism as it makes fundamentalists unduly sensitive and keen to find aberrations in the treatment of cherished concepts, scripture and figures in Islamic consciousness by the minorities. Paradoxically, the law was initially instituted by the British to obviate religious conflict and to promote good understanding and respect among the various religious groups. This should essentially be the *raison d'etre* of such a law. It should foster respect and understanding among people in a multi-religious society like Pakistan to prevent facetious and scurrilous pronouncements on each other's religion. But the Blasphemy Law as it stands does the very opposite. No wonder Abdul Sattar Ghazzali stated, 'The most malignant legacy of Zia is religious extremism which has taken firm roots in our country'. Zia's amendment to the Blasphemy Law is a principal factor in this rise of extremism and intolerance.[32] I.A. Rahim, speaking of the Blasphemy Laws, categorically states: 'Pakistan was a less intolerant society before these laws'.[33] Archbishop Saldhana of Lahore corroborates this view. Recently he said that discrimination against Christians and desecration of church buildings have increased in Pakistan during the last year. Part of this he attributes to the identification of Pakistani Christians with the West, and he said that though Pakistan has received some financial aid from the United States due to its political partnership with the West, its overall affect has been to increase hostility of the Muslim Right to Christians.[34] Shabaz Anwar Bhatti calls the Blasphemy Law a naked sword hanging over Christians.[35] It is evident that Christians find it a constant threat to their security in Pakistan.

It should not however be imagined that only Christians are the victims of false accusations under the Blasphemy Law. Many of the regulations in Section 219 are evidently aimed at the Ahamadiyya. I have already mentioned the case of Tahir Iqbal, a Muslim killed under accusations of blasphemy. *The Christian Voice* points out the instance of one Dr Yunus Sheikh, sentenced to death for blasphemy.[36] Dr Akhtar Hameed Khan, a distinguished social worker, had three times been accused

---

30 Rahim, I.A., 'A critique of Pakistan's Blasphemy Laws', in Tarik Jan, pp. 195-207, p. 199.

31 Ibid.

32 Ghazzali, p. 139.

33 Rahim, I.A., p. 204.

34 *Universe Catholic Newspaper* (3 July 2006).

35 *Pakistan Christian Post* (30 May 2006).

36 *The Christian Voice* (22 August 2004).

of blasphemy, allegedly by a disgruntled former employee, Mr Mobin ud Din, who had been dismissed from employment by Dr Khan from the Orangi Pilot Project founded by him for misappropriation of funds. The employee used the Blasphemy Law as a ruse for his vendetta against Dr Khan, stating that he had blasphemed Islam. It is evident that the Jamat i Islami party colluded with this dishonest individual to bring trumped up charges stating that Dr Khan in an interview to an Indian newspaper had made scurrilous statements against the Prophet. *Takbeer*, a Jamat i Islami organ, published excerpts from this imaginary interview. Though Dr Khan was not convicted, he had been harassed by raids on his house by the police, and even in one case by the army, and detained without warrant or charge.[37] He and his family had been subjected to much emotional trauma by a campaign of vilification by fundamentalist clerics.

Journalists and commentators on Islam are also likely to be victimised if their views on Islam or related matters are liberal or if they subject such matters to critical analysis. Muslim intellectuals such as Fazlur Rahman also run the danger of offending fundamentalists and attracting allegations of blasphemy. In reality, Fazlur Rahman who was initially appointed by Martial Law President General Ayyoub Khan to head the Institute for Islamic Research in Pakistan had to flee the country for voicing thoughts on Qur'anic interpretation that were viewed as radical, heretical and blasphemous by the fundamentalists of Pakistan.

This brings us to the issue of freedom of speech. Article 19 of the Constitution of Pakistan states:

> Every citizen shall have the right to freedom of speech and expression, and there shall be freedom of the press, subject to any reasonable restrictions imposed by law in the interest of the glory of Islam or the integrity, security or defence of Pakistan or any part thereof, friendly relations with foreign States, public order, decency or morality, or in relation to contempt of court or commission of or incitement to an offence. (Constitution of Islamic Republic of Pakistan, 1973)

The clause regarding the 'glory of Islam' is the relevant part of this article for us. This can have a wide interpretation since even a critical analysis of Islamic beliefs, concepts, practice, or *tafsir*[38] can be adjudged to be detrimental to the 'glory of Islam'. So this clause is a potential minefield, giving plenty of latitude for fundamentalists to bring in allegations against well-intentioned scholars writing on Islam. Islamic dogma that since the ninth century all independent thinking and interpretation of scripture has been banned has led to rigidity and narrow thinking in Islamic scholarship. Liberal modern thinkers opine that the gates of *ijtihad* (personal interpretation of the Qur'an) have to be reopened, for Islam to escape this stalemate. Orthodox ulama such as the leaders of the Jamat I Islami or Jamiat Ulema I Islam would be reluctant to concur with this view and would condemn writers and thinkers who proceed to violate this dogma. Received thinking and the *taqlid* (blind imitation) of pre-ninth century scholars seem to be the norm in conventional Islamic

---

37 *Human Rights Watch Publications*, 5/13 (September 19, 1993), 'Persecuted Minorities and Writers in Pakistan'.

38 Exegesis.

thinking. This has led to a stultification of thought, which is the genesis of much of the problems Islam faces in contemporary times, be it the nature of relations with other faiths, the status of women or the application of religious law. The accepted methodology has led to an ossification in Islamic thinking which scholars such as the late Professor Fazlur Rahman would aspire Islam to get out of. This is difficult when power is well entrenched in the hands of orthodox ulama such as those of Pakistan. The Muttahida Majlis Amal being an integral factor of Pakistani power politics, it is difficult for liberal Muslim thinkers to function and disseminate their ideas in Pakistan. A more sophisticated and enlightened population would be receptive to such ideas, but on the whole the Muslim masses of Pakistan are not of this category. The present impasse in Islamo–Western relations and insensitive moves such as the Iraq war has not helped the cause of liberal and reformist Muslim thinkers.

As far as the Qur'an is concerned no Muslim scholar will ever challenge its validity or authenticity. The Qur'an is seen as the word of God and even an intrinsic part of God's being, coeternal with Allah and taken from the Well-Guarded Tablet (Lawah al Mafuz) standing near God's throne. Non-Muslim scholars have however examined the text critically, subjecting it to the same methods of textual critical examination as applied to Christian scripture. I am certain that they cannot do this in Pakistan without blasphemy charges being levelled against them. Muslim scholars may well subject literary critical methods to the Hadith (there is a well-established Islamic science of Hadith Criticism from the medieval days, though the compilations by Bukhari and Muslim are considered to be totally *salih* or sound) and also to *tafsir* (Qur'anic interpretation). The Shari'a can also be subjected to criticism since its sources are not only the Qur'an but also the Ahadith, the deliberations of scholars (*Idjma and Ijtihad*) and methods such as *Quiyas* (analogical reasoning). But with blasphemy laws such as prevailing in Pakistan it is certain that such criticism of the Shari'a, *tafsir* or hadith can very well lead to allegations of blasphemy. Thus freedom of speech and intellectual activity could be severely curtailed by this set of laws, which is a rather iniquitous situation. An instance has been the murder of Naiamat Ahmar, a teacher, poet and writer who was accused of writing blasphemous lines.[39] Naimat Ahmar was in reality a victim of the vengeance of the Manager and some teachers of the High School where he had been Headmaster, whom he had accused of using the high school grounds for personal cultivation and grazing of animals. Ahmar was a Christian, and later on anonymous posters appeared in the school stating that he had vilified the Prophet. Intercession by Bishop John Joseph secured for Mr. Ahmar a transfer to the District Education Office in Faisalabad for his safety, but he was stabbed and killed there in full view of his colleagues by one Farooq, who was convinced that Ahmar had committed the sacrilege he was accused of and therefore according to law merited capital punishment. All Ahmar 's students and many colleagues vouched for his innocence. This is evidently a case of the emboldment of fanatics by a draconian law that imposes capital punishment on offenders. More reprehensible is the fact that many police officers and local clerics congratulated Farooq on his courage and commitment to Islam.

---

39 *AsiaNews.It* (29 May 2006).

Of course the right to free speech has to be tempered by the need to exercise caution. Freedom of speech does not mean that we have a right to insult, offend or wound other people's feelings. The incident of the Danish cartoons is an obvious example. Muslims consider it offensive to publish pictures of the Prophet. This is to avoid compromising the absolute monotheistic belief of Islam. The Prophet is not an object of worship. Islam looks upon him, unlike Jesus in Christianity, as a mere mortal. Pictorial presentations of the Prophet can run the danger of causing idolatry. In addition to this the Danish cartoons insulted the Prophet by presenting him as a terrorist and in other ways. Therefore publishing them in the media was deliberately offensive to Muslims and the right to free speech cannot be an excuse for such actions. But scholarly analysis of the Prophet's life and his words and actions is legitimate and comes under the purview of free speech.

It is interesting that Pakistan has registered a case against the Danish journal *Jyllands Posten* for publishing the cartoons and also against the internet companies Yahoo, Google and Hotmail for allowing access to these drawings. A lawyer petitioned the Supreme Court of Pakistan on behalf of the People's Support Movement. A case was registered against the journal and these companies under the Blasphemy Law. But according to public prosecutor Makhdoom Alikhan it is doubtful that the Blasphemy Law has jurisdiction over material published outside Pakistan.[40] If the cartoons had been published in Pakistan there is no doubt whatsoever that the publisher and the cartoonist would have been convicted and sentenced to the mandatory death penalty.

The Ahamadiyya cannot even use Islamic phrases or terminology, in their religious literature or even personal correspondence. This is a draconian curtailment of freedom of speech indeed!

The genesis of the Blasphemy Law in British India was in the need to prevent public disorder and religious conflict. But the amendments by Zia ul Haqq have diverged from this objective. It is no longer to protect individuals or society from violence but to safeguard the glory and integrity of Islam. This is no doubt a salutary objective, but the validity of accusations under these laws then becomes subjective, interpretative and liable to misinterpretation and even abuse. The old colonial law referred to explicit deeds and scurrilous writing such as happened in the Rangila Rasul case. But in many of the contemporary accusations under the Blasphemy Law the grounds are vague, tenuous and often more imagined than factual.

In Islam the principle of intention is very important and the inner intent is the significant part rather than external action and rituals. For instance, a person might accidentally swallow food during the Ramadan fasting but this does not break the fast. So also in *Salat* or ritual prayer the first action in the ritual cycle is the expression of *Niyyah* or intent. It is strange however that in the Blasphemy Law, though originally there was a clause defining affront to religious sensibilities that has to be deliberate and malicious in intent, this was later dropped so that mere insinuation or innuendo is sufficient to prove the charge. Needless to say this makes the law very ill-defined and liable to misuse.

---

40 See *Pakistan Link News* (27 April 2006).

Journalists have been accused of blasphemy and two newspapers *Mohasib* and *Frontier Post* shut down by the Pakistani regime invoking blasphemy laws.[41] In most such cases no irreverence to Islam, the Prophet or the Qur'an had been intended. Most are based on a fallacious interpretation and reading of articles and other writing. In some cases the writing and actions may cause offence unintentionally as in the case of a sweeper accidentally throwing rubbish on a plaque on which Qur'anic verses had been inscribed. A critical analysis of Islamic concepts that may go against received and orthodox theology may be the grounds for allegations in some instances. Dr Fazlur Rahman was accused on this ground. In some cases the allegations are totally false, and motivated by personal hostility, business rivalry or the need to evict a person from a property.[42]

A tendency to dominate is already existent among the Muslims of Pakistan due to the preponderance of their majority situation. Moreover, as Abdul Sattar Ghazzali states, the Islamicisation of Pakistan by Zia has imbued fanatics with a 'spirit of self-righteousness that is alarming in any civil society'.[43] Blasphemy laws and the like are only likely to exacerbate this feeling and use the laws as tools for domination. This is especially true since the Blasphemy Laws of Pakistan envisage only affront to the religious sensibilities of Muslims. I.A. Rahim opines that such laws are likely to generate demands for harsher laws.[44] It is an escalating phenomenon, the thin end of a wedge. In that case Pakistan is on the slippery slope to religious strife. No wonder *The Christian Voice* stated that the scrapping of Blasphemy Laws would be a first step towards de-institutionalising intolerance.[45] Moreover, it is strange that in a global climate of opinion against capital punishment, through the Blasphemy Law Pakistan has increased the contingencies in which such penalties can be imposed.

Christians of Pakistan have vociferously demanded the scrapping of the Blasphemy Laws. This is mainly because they see it as a perpetual threat to their security and well-being. There is no telling when some Muslim who has cause to bear grudge against them or desire some economic advantage by imprisoning them will come out with a blasphemy accusation. The legal system is favourable to spurious accusations, does not investigate the charges thoroughly as required by the regulations prior to registering a case, and even aid and abet such false accusations. Christians feel that once accusations are brought against them life in Pakistan is not worth living. There can be vigilante action against them resulting in harm to them and their family, or at least they will be *persona non grata* to their Muslim neighbours and friends. The taint of blasphemy accusations do not easily wash away and will blight their entire future life, their employment prospects and their standing in society.

---

41 *IFEX (International Freedom of Expression Exchange)* (12 March 2002).

42 For instance the uprooting of the Christian population from Khanewal in March 1997. See Malik, Iftikhar H., *Islam, Nationalism and the West: Issues of Identity in Pakistan* (London, 1999), p.141.

43 Ghazzali, A.S., p. 239.

44 Rahim, I.A., p. 204.

45 See *The Christian Voice* (20 June 2004): 5.

It was to publicise and highlight this iniquitous situation that Bishop John Joseph of the Catholic diocese of Faisalabad shot himself in front of the Sessions Court of Sahiwal near Lahore on 6 May 1998. Here Ayyoub Masih, a Christian Pakistani, was tried and convicted of blasphemy, his offence being that he had praised Salman Rushdie's novel *The Satanic Verses*. Bishop Joseph's suicide immediately caught the attention of the media and internationalised the plight of Christians in Pakistan. Bishop John Joseph was the founder chairperson of the Justice and Peace Commission of the Roman Catholic Church of Pakistan. He had once organised an inter-denominational rally in Vienna where he had spoken about the plight of Christians in Pakistan and especially the impact of the Blasphemy Laws on them. He had also gone on hunger strikes in the past in support of victims of the Blasphemy Law. The immediate context of his death was the conviction and death sentence on Ayyoub Masih as mentioned earlier. But this might have been the culmination of the cumulative despair and frustration that Bishop John felt about the oppression of Christians and their insecurity due to this ambiguous law. Ayyoub Masih as recounted earlier in this chapter had been shot at by extremists in the court premises itself but had fortunately escaped death.

The Christian community considers Bishop John as a martyr and calls him Shahid John Joseph. An organisation has been formed in his name to help support victims and families of blasphemy accusations. Also a delegation of Christian and Muslim leaders met the Minister for Religious and Minority Affairs after this incident in which the Christians appealed for the abolition of these laws. However, as mentioned earlier the minister Rajah Zafarul Haqq was not in favour of scrapping these laws. He did however set up a Commission for Inter-faith Dialogue which will look into the grievances of minorities and also think of strategies to foster inter-religious harmony. But how effective this Commission is, as Bishop Azariah of Raiwind told me, is yet to be seen. A Christian-Muslim Peace Committee was set up in Faisalabad which it was decided would look into allegations of blasphemy before cases were registered.[46] But whether it has these powers in a statutory sense and has proved effective in preventing spurious allegations is not clear.

Conclusion

The Blasphemy Law by itself is not a malicious law. Its purpose was to strengthen the religious foundations of society, by preventing conflict among religious groups and ensuring their integrity and dignity. Its function should especially be to preserve the honour and dignity and status of religious minorities. In a religiously pluralistic situation the contingency of insulting of religious sensibilities is more on the part of the religious majority than the minorities. But the Blasphemy Law in Pakistan as amended by General Zia ul Haqq has had the very opposite effect. It has made the majority community overly self-conscious and sensitive, embellished their sense of *taqddus* (honour) searching for real or imaginary hurt to such honour and the 'glory of Islam' and gave them a tool for exploiting and oppressing the weak and

---

46 *Asian Human Rights Commission* (15 July 1998).

the vulnerable in the nation, such as the religious minorities and sects. It is also true that the law seems to have given the Muslims the notion that they are a preferred and privileged group in Pakistan, the very antithesis of the aspirations of the founders of Pakistan, who envisaged Pakistan as a modern secular state, a homeland for Indian Muslims but nevertheless where there will be equality for all groups irrespective of religious affiliation. Moreover, it has given the idea to fundamentalists and extremists that they can take the law into their own hands with impunity and take vigilante action and kill even persons exonerated by the courts of infringement of the Blasphemy Law. This development is a perversion of the true purposes of the Blasphemy Law. Therefore it is obvious that there should be far-reaching changes in the structure of the law and its application. Safeguards have to be built in so that it cannot be abused and misused and become a tool of oppression and a threat to the security and rights of religious minorities in Pakistan. If this cannot be done then it is better to do away with this law altogether.

Chapter Six

Islamic resurgence in Pakistan: Bush's war on terror and its aftermath

As I have reiterated throughout this monograph, Pakistan's founders did not envisage the nation to be a theocratic or Islamic state. Their aspiration was to found a state based on secular modernistic ideals, in spite of being created as a homeland for the Muslims of the Indian subcontinent, in which equality of all citizens, their status, rights and privileges including freedom of religion would be paramount. This is why Islamists such as Abul ala Mawdudi did not take kindly to the idea of Pakistan. That the founder's egalitarian ideology was a sound one was later on proved by the secession of East Pakistan from the nation, though they were also in the majority Muslims. The bond of religion did not prove adequate to cementing the relationship in spite of ethnic and cultural differences and distance. The reason was that there was discrimination against the East Pakistanis, and equal opportunities and equal sharing of resources were not ensured between the two regions. Part of the reason for the present problems of Pakistan is that soon after its inception and the death of its founding fathers, Muhammad Ali Jinnah, the Qaid E Azam (father of the nation), and Liaquat Ali Khan, the first Prime Minister of Pakistan, the nation tended to increasing Islamicisation culminating in the martial regime of Zia ul Haqq that witnessed flagrant and overt attempts to Islamicise all aspects of the nation's institutions and public life.

The objective of Islamicising a nation is not necessarily an unsalutory one. The Islamic state has many positive benefits. It offers ideals of morality and ethics far superior to that of secularist ideologies such as capitalism or Marxism. It can promote a life of piety and obedience to God. It can prevent society from lapsing into unmitigated hedonism, the marginalisation of the poor and the weak, rampant commercialisation, consumerism and corporate greed and lack of compassion and neglect of marginalised sections of society. It can promote good family values and respect for elders, which are the cornerstones of any well-ordered society. But it can also promote religious extremism, discrimination of religious minorities in education, employment and such matters, and negation of their religious rights. It can lead to disparities, instil feelings of superiority in one community over the others, and create problems of how to apply religious law that is based on the tenets of one religion to others who are not its adherents, though the underlying spirit of Islam as defined by the Prophet is egalitarianism, The Qur'an states 'Verily the most honoured of you in the sight of God is the most righteous of you' (Qur'an 49:13). There is some truth in what Tarik Jan states of the Islamic state:

The Islamic state is not adversarial to civil society. The tension between law and the individual or the never-ending conflict between the societal good and individual rights so often the case in secular societies is mostly non-existent in an Islamic state; for the Shari'ah, contrary to man-made laws, is held sacrosanct both by the state and its citizens.[1]

The last part of her statement is, however, too sanguine, and can compare to that of Ayatollah Khomeini when he said that there is no need for a police force in an Islamic state to enforce laws as the people will be ready to obey the laws of God without being coerced into it. The realities of life in Iran have not justified his expectations. Elsewhere Tarik Jan states:

> Secularism decomposes religion since it empties God of his authority.... (It) replaces God with an idolatry of the masses who combines in themselves the ruler as well as the ruled.[2]

She alleges that the separation of the state and religion which has happened in Western nations is an outcome of the Christian monastic trend of renouncing the world. It is well known that Prophet Muhammad abhorred monasticism. He stated '*La rabbaniyya fi Islam*' (There is no monkery in Islam). Tarik Jan seems to contend that the holistic nature of Islam cannot envisage the separation of religion and politics; relegating religion to the private sphere is not possible in Islamic societies.

One of the salient features of Islam in modern times has been the ascendancy of a strict strait-laced type of Islam in many Muslim nations, which has led to both a resurgence in devotion and faith but also in many ways repression, and cessation of personal interpretation and flexibility for new approaches to belief and practice in the Islamic world. Not all these movements are related to Wahabism or Salafism but the ideology of Wahabism has been central to this Islamic resurgence. Wahabism can be likened to a Lutheran reformation in Islam as far as it seeks to purify Islam of some superstitious practices such as found in the Sufi expressions of Islam. A central feature of Wahabism is that it seeks a reversion to an Islam of the Prophet's days and aims to expunge later accretions. It is also associated with the Arab idea in Islam. In reality, Islam has transcended national and ethnic boundaries, and there is much heterogeneity of practice gained as it interacted with cultures other than Arab, though the essential belief and practice remains the same all over the world – for instance *tawhid*, monotheism or the *Ibadah*, the six pillars of Islamic practice. But Wahabism extols the pristine purity of the Islam of the Prophet's days, which inevitably was Arab in character. Thus the enrichment of Islam as it spread to other regions of the world and absorbed some of the indigenous customs and traditions are anathema to the Wahabis, who sought to propagate actively in non-Arab Islamic societies the need to expunge these cultural accretions from the practice of Islam and restore it to the pristine purity of the Islam of the Prophet's days. Adoration of saints and martyrs, belief in and performance of miracles, belief in the *ijaz* (inimitability) of the Prophet's companions and even the celebration of the Prophet's birthday

---

1   Jan, Tarik, 'Questioning the Blasphemy Laws', in Jan, Tarik (ed.), *Pakistan between Secularism and Islam: Ideology, Issues and Conflict* (Islamabad, 1998), pp. 241-56, p. 243.

2   Jan, Tarik, Introduction, p. 8.

(*Mawlid un Nabi*) were decried. The Sufi ritual of *dhikr* with accompanying music and thaumaturgical acts of self-mortification was rejected. Many of these were categorised as *bida* (innovation) and *shirk* (polytheism). The financial viability of Saudi Arabia, the land of the main proponents of Wahabism, has been a factor in the spread of this ideology. The fact that the principal shrines of Islam are in Saudi Arabia and that annually millions of Muslims from all over the world go there, and also that many ulama are trained in Saudi Wahabi institutions are also factors in the spread of this puritanical form of Islam. However, the worldwide propagation of the many varieties of Wahabism has led to greater commitment to Islamic belief and practice in many parts of the world, and thus led to a global Islamic resurgence. The Taliban of Afghanistan is an extreme case of strict application of orthodox Islamic law and paradigm of the Wahabi model of Islamic ideology. But in many other Muslim societies the greater fervour for adhering to rituals, Islamic dress and shunning of adaptation from non-Islamic cultures or Westernisation is mainly fuelled by this Wahabi type of reformation.

This Islamic resurgence has not passed Pakistan by. The germs of this ideology had already been present there since the nation's inception in 1947. With the passing of the secularists Jinnah and Liaquat Ali Khan from the helm of power the ground had been prepared for the spread of the Wahabi type of ideology with greater ease. Abul Ala Mawdudi, an Islamist ideologue, highly regarded in both India and Pakistan, and who migrated to Pakistan in the wake of partition, subscribed to the Wahabi ideology. Zulfikar Ali Bhutto was the only politician of note to succeed Jinnah and Liaquat Ali Khan. Educated in Berkeley he was a confirmed secularist and seemed to be attuned to the secularist ideology of the nation's founders. Bhutto was an idealist, had a genuine interest in democratising Pakistan and relieving poverty, but his measures achieved very little success. His idealism therefore gave way to pragmatism and he played the religious card and tried to appease the fundamentalists. When he came under pressure from the religious parties to prove his Islamic credentials he had to accede to measures which his instinct would have told him were not in Pakistan's best interests. He declared the Ahamadiyya to be non-Muslim, a measure which Jinnah had resisted tooth and claw. This was a serious mistake and Bhutto suffered the consequences when Zia ul Haqq, a rampant Muslim fundamentalist in the guise of a uniformed general, grabbed power and instituted measures that led Pakistan irretrievably away from the secular path.

In my previous chapters, I have delineated clearly how Zia, by totally undemocratic measures and the introduction of oppressive laws such as the Blasphemy Law and the Hudood Laws, sought to achieve this and how he pushed Muslim fundamentalists and obscurantist mullahs into positions of power and privilege, and how he compromised the judicial system. Many of the Madrassas in Pakistan are funded by Saudi Arabia and staffed by Ulama of the Wahabi persuasion so this ideology has really obtained a strong foothold in Pakistan now. We must remember that right from the earliest days of the nation the influence of secularists such as Jinnah was countered by Islamic ideologues of Pakistan such as Mawdudi who had a Wahabi orientation in their teaching and praxis of Islam.

Unfortunately, it was at this critical juncture another significant development occurred in world politics. This was the invasion of Afghanistan in 1979 by the

Soviet Union to shore up an unpopular and minority Marxist regime. The United States of America saw in this an opportunity to humiliate the Soviet Union, foist a Vietnam type of conflict there and promote American objectives in the cold war. To this end the USA supported pragmatically the *mujahideen* or holy warriors. In this America compromised entirely its ideals of secularism, and helped foster the long-term hegemony of religious fundamentalism not only in Afghanistan but also in Pakistan for which the USA and the world and particularly Pakistan would have to pay dearly later. Not only because Zia, fundamentalist undemocratic ruler, became indispensable to the USA, but it caused the emergence of the Taliban, literally religious scholars, who took up arms in the cause of Islam and against secularism in Afghanistan. Pakistan now became a front-line state actively engaged in promoting and aiding the fight against Marxism in Afghanistan.

The Soviet debacle in Afghanistan and its withdrawal did not bring stability and peace to Afghanistan and the region as perhaps expected by the USA and Pakistan, but Afghanistan lapsed into internecine warfare among factions of the Mujahideen, mainly based on ethnicity, who had fought the Marxists. Of these, the Pushtun Taliban emerged triumphant, controlling a major portion of Afghan territory. The aftermath was not good for Afghanistan and its denizens especially for the women, since the Taliban instituted a particularly rigorous implementation of Islamic law and enforced it forcibly and even cruelly, alienating world opinion. To the Taliban democracy and respecting individual rights was a Western institution and mode of governance, so they rejected it in favour of a theocracy. For Pakistan the consequences were even more horrific. When the Soviets withdrew, Pakistan was practically abandoned by the United States and had to contend with numerous problems. The mujahideen and the Mullahs who supported them had an aggressive ideology that was totally fundamentalist and non-secular. Pakistan as a modern nation was left with this problem on its hands. As Hassan Abbas states, these mujahideen who had been fully switched on to fight a holy war against the Soviets could not switch themselves off. Pakistan also faced a massive refugee problem.[3] The attention of the obscurantist madrassas financed by Saudi money now turned to internal politics in Pakistan. Moreover, Islamic fundamentalists had been supported by the Pakistani army leadership including the Commander in Chief and Martial Law Administrator Zia himself, and also by the Intelligence Services. The top brass of the army had gained financially from the war and the monetary support that was coming from the coffers of the United States and Saudi Arabia. So this did not augur well for both democracy and secularism in Pakistan, as well as maintenance of peace and stability. A drastic reorientation of the army and the body politic was imperative and even now the present ruler of Pakistan has to contend with this problem. President Musharaff has his hands full and has to tread a fine line so as not to upset the Mullahs and Islamic rightist parties, while maintaining the principles of fairness and impartiality between ethnic and religious communities.

The ISI (Inter-Services Intelligence) wing of the Pakistan Army had all along promoted and aided the Jihadis. They and the CIA had both financed the mujahideen and set up training camps not only in Afghanistan but also in Pakistan. The Kashmir

---

3   Abbas, Hassan, *Pakistan's drift into Extremism* (New York, 2005), p. 11.

issue with India has been a long-standing problem and initially the ISI had promoted insurgency in the Indian part of Kashmir (called Indian Occupied Kashmir or IOK by Pakistanis) and also infiltration of armed Jihadis from Pakistan and the Pakistani part of Kashmir (called Azad Kashmir, i.e. Free Kashmir, by Pakistan and Pakistan Occupied Kashmir or POK by India) into IOK. And when the Afghan war erupted there were Jihadis involved in both the Kashmir confrontation with India and the Afghan conflict. With the end of the Soviet occupation many of the Jihadis turned their full attention to Kashmir, not only Kashmiri and Pakistani jihadis but also the remnants of militants from the Afghan war. Afghans and other mujahideen from all parts of the world had amassed in the region under the leadership of Bin Laden and Mullah Omar. The ISI was not aware that they were creating a monster which they would not be able to control in the future and would be a menace to peace and stability in Pakistan itself. The ISI and the Pakistan army, according to Abbas, suffered from the inertia and malaise of any large bureaucratic organisation and disregarded this danger.[4] So a moderate and progressive leader like Musharaff found himself not fully able to reorient the army or control the growing strength and influence of the Jihadis in Pakistan.

The attacks on the World Trade Center and the Pentagon on 11 September 2001 were significant events in the global scene that set in motion many trends and conflicts in the world. Bush's response to this was ill-conceived and not well thought out. The al Qaeda is not a nation state but Bush's almost instinctive response was to attack a state. That is of course the easier response than to investigate the affiliations and networking of the perpetrators of this atrocity. Afghanistan was the most likely candidate since it was on the whole ruled by the Taliban whose repressive implementation of the Shari'a had alienated world opinion, exacerbated by the gross bigotry of destroying a world heritage, the Bamiyan Buddhist sculptures. And the Taliban and its leader Mullah Omar sheltered Osama bin Laden, said to be the leader and mastermind of al Qaeda (The Base), an amorphous and global Islamic Jehadi entity alleged to be behind the 11 September attacks. World opinion was not against the invasion of Afghanistan, but the Iraq war was a different matter. The needlessness and the lies surrounding the rationale for the invasion of Iraq, such as non-existent weapons of mass destruction, the fact that Saddam Hussain, unlike the Taliban, was not an Islamic fundamentalist, and the growing suspicion that there were other agendas behind the Iraq war alienated the sympathies of the Muslim world and others from the US administration's venture.

The war in Afghanistan also has not achieved much. The Taliban and its leadership have not been destroyed and have regrouped in strength and now control many areas in Southern Afghanistan.[5] Osama bin Laden and Mullah Omar are at large. Al Qaeda is very active in the region.

Zia ul Haqq's policies had ensured that the fundamentalists and the Jihadis had grown in strength in Pakistan, bolstered by financial help from the CIA, Saudi Arabia and the ISI. Many of them had moved to positions of power, not through a democratic

---

4   Ibid., p. 13.

5   See Journo, Elan, 'Washington's failed war in Afghanistan', http://www.enterstageright. com (6 November 2006).

process but with the patronage of the Martial Law Administrator. But later on they have developed independent means to finance themselves and are now a growing force in Pakistani politics. The Afghanistan and Iraq wars, especially the latter, had been responsible mainly for the growing popularity of the Islamic militants. So of late the Mullahs have been returned to the national and provincial legislatures in strength. This could be seen as a rebuff to President Bush, and President Musharaff's pro-US policies. In fact, both the Afghan and the Iraq wars have failed to realise their objectives of bringing stability and genuine democracy to these regions. They have only exacerbated the internecine warfare among various ethnic groups in the two regions which paradoxically had been better controlled under the dictatorial regimes of Saddam Hussain and Mullah Omar. The enormous loss of life, including innocent civilians such as children and women, in both countries and the continuing chaos have proved to be a recruiting sergeant for militants not only in these places but also in Pakistan. The atrocities committed by US troops in Iraq, torture and illegal imprisonment in Guantanamo Bay and 'extraordinary rendition', i.e. transporting by the US of political prisoners to countries where torture is permissible, such actions have angered even moderate Muslims in Pakistan. Even the substantial financial help by Bush, such as cancellation of debts, has not helped change the people's mindset in favour of the USA. Some of this anger against the USA has rubbed off on other nations of the West and even on the Christian community of Pakistan.[6] But according to Bishop Azariah though there is a critical attitude to the Iraq war and general ill-feeling towards the US it has not impacted too adversely on the Christians of Pakistan.

Abbas points out what he calls a paradigm shift in the equation of power.[7] Traditionally, the army has wielded power in Pakistan but according to Abbas now the fundamentalists are increasingly seen to be the axis of power in Pakistan. This restricts Musharaff's programme of reforms and also has gathered forces against him which threaten his authority and even his life. Dr Ayman al-Zawahiri, Osama bin Laden's top aide, exhorted Pakistanis openly not to tolerate Musharaff whom he described as a traitor to Islam and an ally of Crusader America and the Hindus.[8] Apparently even in the top echelons of the Pakistani army there is dissatisfaction with Musharaff and his liberal and pro-Western policies.[9] Musharaff's military action against the Taliban and militant Islamic elements in the Afghan-Pakistani border has caused him to be branded as a traitor to Islam.

The Kashmir issue, the Afghan War and now the Iraq war have therefore spawned a number of extremist organisations in Pakistan apart from the Muttahida Majlis Amal and such rightist Islamic parties which are more respectable and seen as legitimate political parties, though their attitude is as anti-Western and anti-Christian as the others, and they also have an agenda of restricting both religious rights and human rights in spite of their apparent respectability. But these parties are anyway willing to work through the ballot box rather than with force of arms. The Jihadi

---

6   *Boston Globe* (10 October 2006).
7   Abbas, p. 14.
8   Mir, Amir, *The True Face of Jehadis* (Lahore, 2004), p. 42.
9   Ibid., p. 45.

parties are different in their orientation. There is a plethora of them in Pakistan and it has made the region the hotbed of extremism in the world.

Bush's so-called war on terrorism is an ill-conceived project that has only served to increase terrorism in places where it was hitherto unknown, for instance in Iraq and in the United Kingdom. Iraq under Saddam Hussain was only nominally Muslim, since the dictator was hardly a fervent Muslim and certainly not a fundamentalist of the ilk of Khomeini or Mullah Omar. His was an oppressive regime and he sought personal aggrandisement, building palaces and living an opulent life-style. He sought fearsome weapons of war and in his invasion of Kuwait betrayed Napoleonic ambitions. He sought to impose discipline in ethnically pluralist Iraq by adopting dire measures such as draining the marshes in southern Iraq peopled by rebellious Shia who were to some extent under the control of Iran. He gassed the fractious Kurds. The fact that Saddam was a secularist irked Iran which did not like a ruler with such an ideology so near its vicinity. This led to the eight-year conflict between the two. The present internecine strife in Iraq reveals the extent of its ethnic problem and perhaps justifies to some extent Saddam's repressive measures to impose some semblance of internal order in that divided country.

Toppling Saddam and instituting a sort of democratic government there under the aegis of US and other occupying forces in Iraq have not proved successful in restoring order and harmony to the country. The Iraqi government is not a government of moderates. Some of its members are themselves extremists and lead extremist factions, both Sunni and Shi'a, which are bent upon killing each other.[10] A nation which had no place in the annals of terrorism now attracts terrorists like flies to the honey pot. Moreover, the unfortunate participation in the Iraq war by Prime Minister Blair has induced terrorist activities in the United Kingdom, a nation which, in spite of its colonial past and collaboration in the creation of Israel, has so far been respected by Muslims as a just and fair-minded nation, prudent and judicious in its involvement in foreign affairs. The war on terrorism has exacerbated Islamic militancy and extremism, has led to repressive measures such as detention without trial in the United States and the United Kingdom, restrictions on civil liberties and invasion of the privacy of its citizens and a general atmosphere of fear and suspicion. This project was undertaken without identifying and considering solutions for the rise of Islamic fundamentalism and extremism. It was almost as though the violence of Islamic radicalism could be countered by greater violence against them. But the extremists, misguided though they are, are fighting for causes beyond the normal rather pragmatic objectives, they are fighting for *din*, their religion, and for Allah, and for the preservation according to them of their beliefs, their religious law and even their identity as Muslims. So they do not mind self-immolation in the process. It is difficult to fight an enemy who does not care about personal safety or the preservation of life. There are many a disillusioned youngster, frustrated in life by unemployment, plagued by poverty and illiteracy, in Palestine to whom being a *Shahid*, martyr for their faith, is a *cause celebre*, and whose parents often approve

---

10 See Galbraith, Peter W., 'The case for dividing Iraq', in *Time* (13 November 2006): 30-4, 33.

and are even ready to send more and more of their sons into the war with what they consider as the Djall, the hated United States, or Israel.

Many aver that the cold war has now been replaced by a conflict between the liberal and democratic values of the West and the fundamentalist and oppressive values of Islam. The war between capitalism and socialism has now been replaced by this new clash of ideologies. But Lamin Sanneh in a very perceptive article states:

> It is difficult in the now well known outcome of the Cold War to believe that Islamic radicalism has any similarity with the ill-fated Soviet Union. The fundamentalists are not a state or an empire, though they hanker after a similitude of one such. Too, their blue print is not a messianic classless society or a workers' commune, but instead the truth of God divinely mandated.... How would you confront or contain a foe like that? The Cold War analogy, for that reason, is unilluminating, and merely throws us off the scent.[11]

It is evident that in Bush's time Islam is more and more looked upon as a danger to the United States and perhaps to the Western world. It was as though a green menace was replacing the red menace of communism. Some of this Islamophobia was fed by writers such as Steven Emerson, Daniel Pipes and Bernard Lewis. Samuel Huntingdon's well-known clash of civilisations thesis, which he has now recanted, also exacerbated this idea of Islam being a menace to Western civilisation, values and traditions. Though the Muslims of America were very supportive of Bush in the Presidential election it is observable that he gradually let them down and, as already evident in Israel, the US also joined the trend of demonising Islam. Right wing Christians are an important constituency for Republicans and these Christians abandoned all subtlety in vilifying Islam. Yvonne Haddad writes:

> The right wing Christian community had already shifted its interpretation of the signs of the end times after the Israeli victory of 1967. Included among the signs was now a major battle between Muslims and Jews restored to Israel, a cataclysmic event that will herald the imminent return of the Messiah.... Millenarian Christians welcomed the intensification of conflict between the two faiths since it would mean the final redemption of the Jews and urged Israel to hold firm. Their preachers, casting away all pretence at political correctness, engaged in demonising Islam and its Prophet with gusto reminiscent of the discourses that launched the Crusades and justified European colonisation of Muslim nations.[12]

The half-hearted way in which Bush approaches the issue of the peace process between Israel and Palestine does not go down well with the Islamic Ummah. Bush seems to be adopting a *laissez-faire* policy as far as the Palestinian issue is concerned but on the other hand pursuing vigorously the conquest of Afghanistan and Iraq. World opinion was not so much against the subjugation of the Taliban because of their excesses in implementing a strict code of Islamic law, especially where women

---

11 Sanneh, Lamin, 'Shariah sanctions and state enforcement: A Nigerian Islamic debate and intellectual critique', in Geaves, Gabriel, Haddad and Smith (eds), *Islam and the West Post 9/11* (Aldershot, 2004), pp. 146-65, p. 147.

12 Haddad, Yvonne, 'The shaping of a moderate North American Islam: between 'Mufti' Bush and 'Ayatollah' Ashcroft', in Geaves, Gabriel, Haddad and Smith, pp. 97-114, p. 104.

were concerned, and the holding of public executions and the destruction of the world heritage site of the Bamiyan Buddhas. But the Iraq war attended by devious arguments, the haste to topple Saddam, the sidelining and denigrating of the United Nations on this issue and manipulation of intelligence seemed to indicate that there were other pragmatic agenda behind the onslaught against Iraq, though overtly the whole project was couched in idealistic language. Muslims all over the world were incensed by what they considered as unnecessary interference in the internal affairs of an Islamic nation, removing of a Muslim head of state, occupation of a distant land which was no direct threat to US security, and where Islamic radicalism and terrorism were not particularly noticeable. Moreover, the invasion of Iraq and its aftermath that were attended by terrible loss of life, atrocities such as US troops firing indiscriminately on the civilian population and abuse of prisoners, and the continued neglect of the Palestinian problem, are construed by Muslims as an onslaught against their sovereignty and even against the religion of Islam itself. Thus the region attracted large numbers of extremists and fanatics bent upon getting rid of what they perceived as colonial occupation and an affront to their religion. The installation of a regime in Iraq, though apparently attended by democratic process, has not been able to quell civil unrest and inter-ethnic conflict. The institution of a government under these circumstances seemed to many to be contrived and not genuinely representative of the people of Iraq, while it was totally ineffective in bringing peace and stability to the nation.

The Muslims of Pakistan that include substantial numbers of reasonable, moderate and even enlightened individuals were on the whole aggrieved by the policies of the US and its allies in Iraq. It is inevitable that the Islamic fundamentalists would be totally opposed to the invasion of Iraq and the happenings in Palestine, but now they had the support of the usually silent moderate majority as well. In recent elections for the first time the fundamentalists have done well. Extremist organisations such as the Jamat al Dawah (MDI) and the Lahskar E. Toiba have declared their intentions to attack the intellectual elite of Pakistan as well as Americans and Indians.[13] Thus the situation in Pakistan, as I should imagine in many another Muslim nation, is becoming critical. Pakistan had for years posed as an ally of the US and the West, mostly to counter the pro-Soviet polices of the Indian government, and also to extract as much aid from the West as possible to shore up its ailing economy, but now this is becoming increasingly difficult. President Musharaff has the difficult task of treading a fine line between appeasing the US and its allies in the West and of not provoking the sensibilities of Pakistani Muslims unduly. The al Qaeda has openly branded Musharaff a traitor and called for his assassination. Many analysts have called Musharaff's moves against the fundamentalists and extremists half-hearted, but he is probably trying to find a balance between coming down too hard on them and alienating public opinion and containing their excesses as much as possible. Musharaff has proved himself, particularly in his dealing with India, to be a good statesman and one, who though he came to power by a coup d'état, is more measured and thoughtful in his policies and actions than many a democratically elected leader.

---

13 Abbas, p. 215.

The Jihadi outfits generally consider the Pakistani administration to be on the side of Christians, Hindus and Jews. They aver that the usual convention of obtaining consent from the rulers before engaging in jihad does not therefore apply to them. They emphasise the un-Islamic character of the ruler of Pakistan, which gives them a free licence to exercise their discretion in their actions. They now have a certain amount of financial independence and therefore the army and the ISI which in the past had a measure of say and control in their operations have lost such privileges.

While we are talking about Jihadi outfits it will be appropriate to say a few words about the term 'Jihad'. Jihad literally means struggle or striving, not holy war. So any form of struggle is jihad, not necessarily in the sphere of physical conflict. The Prophet while returning from a battle mentioned 'we are now turning from the lesser jihad to the greater jihad' meaning that the internal struggle in the human mind against evil is actually the more important jihad than physical battle. Jihad is essentially defensive warfare. Permission was given to the believers in Medina when they were attacked by a vastly superior force of the Quraish to defend themselves in an armed struggle. Sura 22:39 states: 'To those against whom war is made permission is given (to fight) because they are wronged.' So the permission for jihad seems to be a concession from God in an exigent situation.

Jihad is primarily in defence of religion, i.e. one's faith and God, not for personal aggrandisement or conquest of territory. It is also for defending the weak and the oppressed. So Jihad is *Jihad fi sabil Allah* (Struggle in the cause of Allah). Some of the Jihadi outfits in Pakistan now state that jihad is offensive defence,[14] suggesting pre-emptive offensive, but this a departure from the classical definition of Jihad, which allows jihad only when one is attacked. The primary concern is to effect peace between hostile factions, not to kill or exact revenge. 'Make peace between them (the two fighting groups), but if one of the two persists in aggression against the other, fight the aggressors until they revert to God's commandment' (Sura 49:9). Certain norms apply when engaging in jihad. The Qur'an states: 'And fight in the way of Allah those who fight you, but transgress not the limits. Truly, Allah likes not the transgressors' (Sura 2:190).

The Prophet's prescriptions regarding jihad are even more explicit:

> Do not betray; do not carry grudges; do not deceive; do not mutilate; do not kill children; do not kill the elderly; do not kill women; do not destroy beehives or burn them; do not cut down fruit bearing trees; do not slaughter sheep, cattle or camels except for food.[15]

It is obvious that the actions of most of the Jihadi organisations are not compliant with either the Qur'an or the Hadith.

Though based on erroneous interpretations of the Qur'an and even contravening its teachings, Jihadi outfits flourish in Pakistan. Bush's failed foreign policy, especially the wrong way it has gone about tackling the terror menace, has enabled the radicals, fundamentalists and extremists to garner support in Pakistan. They could have been effectively marginalised and contained if the moderate, enlightened sections of Pakistani Muslims were not alienated by the excesses and illegal and

---

14 Ibid.
15 From a hadith [saying] of Prophet Muhammad through Abu Bakr.

unjust actions of the Bush-Blair combine and their ally Israel in the Middle East. The actions of Israel in Lebanon and how Bush and Blair were reluctant to intervene or advise and caution Israel in its heinous and wanton destruction of Lebanon and massacre of innocent civilians have made the Muslim Umma consider both the USA and the United Kingdom to be inimical to Islam, callous and not averse to Israeli high-handed actions. Amir Ul Azim, Secretary in Lahore of the Jamat I Islami, an important Islamist party of Pakistan said: 'People hate America as a whole. People in general think the West, and Bush especially, have a double standard for Muslims. They are killing Muslims. *It can come to the point where it can affect the relationship between the Muslim community and the Christian community*'[16] (italics mine). For instance, apparently Christian hospitals supported by US finance though providing optimal health care and facilities are boycotted by the majority of Pakistani Muslims,[17] in spite of the fact that in the government healthcare institutions the standard is far from desirable and even appalling at times.

Pakistan has unfortunately been embroiled in two significant crises in its recent history, the conflict in Afghanistan and the Kashmir issue. It could not stay neutral or aloof from the first – Afghanistan being its immediate neighbour and a number of Pakistanis being of Pushtun ethnicity in the northwestern frontier region bordering with Afghanistan. These Pathans (as they are often called) have considerable loyalty and fellow feeling with their Pushtun compatriots in Afghanistan. A number of the Taliban and even Mullah Omar, the Taliban leader, and Osama bin Laden the Saudi Arabian leader of al Qaeda are suspected to be in hiding in this region of Pakistan, harboured by its Pushtun citizens. Pakistan has therefore been inevitably drawn into the traumatic happenings in Afghanistan, initially on the side of the Taliban when the latter were in the graces of the United States, and now against them. President Musharaff has launched a vigorous military campaign against the Taliban and al Qaeda militias in Waziristan, the mountainous region in the Afghan-Pakistan border and ideal terrain for use as a hideout for militants. This has not gone down well with the Islamic groups in Pakistan and many have condemned Musharaff's strikes, such as the one which killed a large number of apparently innocent religious students in a Madrassa. They consider Musharaff's actions as an ally of President Bush in his war on terror as a betrayal of Islam.

The Kashmir issue is one which is found to be extremely difficult to resolve. The problem originated with the inception of Pakistan and was caused by the secession of Kashmir to India by its Dogra Hindu king in 1947. The issue was forced by Pathans supported by Pakistan who tried to wrest control of Kashmir. Prime Minister Nehru of India refused to intervene until the Maharajah signed a treaty of accession to India. India's action could be seen as opportunistic. A portion of Kashmir is now held by Pakistan and another small portion by China. India argues that the whole region belongs to it by virtue of the Maharajah's action, and does not consider Kashmir as disputed territory. Indian intransigence regarding the Kashmir issue has ensured that this is a cancer that generates mutual hostility and recrimination between India and Pakistan.

---

16 Quoted in *The Boston Globe* (10 October 2006).
17 Ibid.

It is not clear now that the majority of Kashmiris, though of the Muslim faith, wish to accede to India or Pakistan. They might want independence from both. India initially gave considerable autonomy to Kashmir, calling their political leader Sheikh Abdallah Prime Minister of Kashmir. India later withdrew this special status and now considers Kashmir as one of the states of the Indian Union. It refuses any foreign mediation or the internationalisation of the Kashmir issue, considering it purely as an internal matter.

The independence of Kashmir from India is an objective that drives many an Islamic radical to infiltrate the Indian-held Kashmir region and attack Indian forces there. Whatever may be the pros and cons of Kashmiri political status the fact remains that the Kashmir controversy is the genesis of considerable Islamic militancy in Pakistan and the force that animates many of the Jihadi outfits there.

The Jaish e Muhammad, formed by Maulana Mazhood Azar is one of the nascent Jihadi groups in Kashmir. The Maulana became popular after he was arrested while in Kashmir in 1994 on a mission. The Indian authorities released him as part of a prisoner exchange in connection with the highjacking of an Indian Airliner in 1999. On his release Mazhood formed this new organisation Jaish e Muhammad (Army of the Prophet Muhammad). Jaish e Muhammad is based in Pakistan and has as its objective the ouster of Indian forces from Jammu and Kashmir. It also has dreams of taking control of the Babri Masjid in Ayodhya, the focus of a bitter Hindu-Muslim controversy, and even Amritsar, the capital of Indian Punjab.

The Jaish e Muhammad has been considerably weakened of late due to the shift in policy of the Pakistan Government led by President Musharaff. It had been actively abetted by the ISI but has lost its support under Musharaff. It was also implicated in the assassination attempts on the President and consequently discredited. It has now reportedly split into two groups.

The Lashkar e Toiba is however a Jihadi group that continues to be optimistic about its future in spite of President Musharaff assuring India that Pakistani territory would not be used for terrorist activity in Kashmir. Amir Mir states that the Pakistan establishment has agreed not to interfere with the recruitment and training of cadres by Lashkar e Toiba, and collection of funds if they lie low and do not criticise President Musharaff's actions.[18] How authentic this information is is not certain. It is true however that at Mudrike in the Punjab the Jihadi activities of the Lashkar e Toiba such as training of militants continue unabated. They still distribute pamphlets outside mosques preaching jihad against Russia, India and Israel.[19] The Harkatul Mujahideen and the Hizbul Mujahideen are two other organisations which have the objective of liberating Kashmir from Indian occupation as well as the freeing of other regions where Muslims are viewed as oppressed.

For us the relevance of the numerous Jihadi groups in Pakistan is that though their operations are in the main directed against other states such as India and in general the USA and Israel, their hostility can easily turn against religious minorities like the Christians, the Shi'a and the Ahamadiyya. Moreover they are groups whose ultimate objective is to make Pakistan a theocratic state. Some have vowed to undertake jihad

---

18 Amir, p. 96.
19 Ibid., p. 101.

to turn Pakistan into a pure Islamic state. They categorise intellectual Muslims, the Western-oriented elite and the politicians of Pakistan as corrupt and ungodly. So the move is towards the classical definition of the Islamic state with the state machinery in the hands of ulama rather than elected politicians, and intellectual analysis of religious matters and issues decried while unquestioning acceptance of the decrees of the ulama is advocated. Therefore their activities are directed not only externally against other nations but also internally against those whom they consider as opposed to the formation of a 'pure' Islamic state in Pakistan. That includes moderates such as President Musharaff and religious minorities such as the Christians who are also opposed to the creation of an Islamic state in Pakistan.

The escalating terrorist activities and ascendancy of hardline and militant Muslim parties and Jihadi outfits in Pakistan do not augur well for good inter-religious relations there. The failed foreign policy of the US and its allies has proved detrimental to the Christians and moderates in Pakistan. The hostility against Christians is bound to escalate unless there is a radical shift in US policies and its actions in Iraq. Otherwise the forces for Islamicising Pakistan will gather strength and support and this will lead to the oppression of Christians and other religious minorities there. As long as President Musharaff is in power we can expect a certain measure of stability and restraining of Islamic militants. If he falls, the political scene in Pakistan is bound to descend to chaos and this will prove extremely hazardous for minorities, especially the already beleaguered Christian minority of Pakistan.

Chapter Seven

Movements for inter-religious dialogue in Pakistan

The previous chapters perhaps paint a gloomy and depressing picture of Christian-Muslim relations in Pakistan. The general hostility to Christians, misrepresentation of Christianity and Christians in textbooks, discrimination in employment, prohibition on Christian evangelisation, such circumstances do not augur well for good Christian-Muslim relations in Pakistan. However, there are some rays of hope in this dark situation. Movements for enhancing the rapport between the two communities are not totally non-existent. One sanguine circumstance is the attitude of enlightened and educated Muslims in Pakistan. The academics, editors and Imran Khan, the noted cricketer and politician, that I met all spoke in terms of the importance of developing good communal relations in Pakistan and gave realistic assessments of the abuses to which the Blasphemy Law, for instance, has been put to in oppressing the minorities. I do not think they were merely paying lip-service, but seemed to be genuinely desiring good rapport between religious communities in their country. The writings by Muslim intellectuals which I examined, examples of which we have seen in earlier chapters, also reveal that they are desirous of inter-faith dialogue and amity in the nation, and a fair and just treatment of minorities. Fr. Joe Paul writes that the enlightened sections of Pakistanis such as artists, poets, journalists, lawyers, and doctors are involved in the struggle for eradicating extremism.[1]

As a matter of fact there is much potential for good Muslim-Christian relations. The two faiths share common patriarchs, prophets and historical antecedents. Jesus is a highly exalted figure in Islam as well as Christianity. Isa Nabi, as he is called in Islam, is a revered prophet to Muslims, and the Qur'an mentions his name often. Muslims believe in the virgin birth of Jesus and the miracles that he wrought during his ministry, including the creation of life and making birds of clay alive, which does not find a place in the canonical gospels. Jesus is described as a word, a spirit and a sign to the children of Israel in the Qur'an, which strangely echo the Christian concepts surrounding Jesus. Though Islam does not go beyond describing Jesus as a prophet in the long line of prophets commencing with Adam and ending with Muhammad, these depictions of Jesus in the Qur'an make him out to be a super-human figure. Of course, the absolute monotheism of Islam prevents it from describing Jesus as an incarnation of God, or as the Son of God. They do not believe in the death of Jesus on the Cross. These are stumbling blocks to Christian-Muslim dialogue but there is enough common ground to serve as stepping-stones to such an encounter.

---

1 *The Christian Voice* (5 September 2004): 1.

As a matter of fact the Qur'an categorically states that Christians and Muslims are good friends. Sura 5:85 states that:

Strongest among men in enmity
To the believers wilt thou
Find the Jews and pagans;
And nearest among them in love
To the believers wilt thou
Find those who say
'We are Christians'.

The Sura goes on to state that Christians will also find a place in Paradise on Judgement Day.

It is mystifying how two religions which share so much and have such potential for dialogue and harmony have in the past and even now been involved in violence against each other and bear mutual hostility.

The Government of Pakistan has also instituted some measures for safeguarding the interests of minorities. The present administration is sympathetic to their concerns and is ready to listen to them and is generally desirous of treating them fairly. But the increasing popularity of the fundamentalists and extremists in the nation acts against the good intentions of the government being implemented effectively. The war on Iraq and the Palestinian situation have exacerbated hostility against the West and Christians, who the Muslims erroneously see as the allies of the West. The moderate majority cannot make their voices heard effectively in this emotionally charged atmosphere. The voice of reason is drowned out in the clamour against the atrocities we see happening daily in Palestine, in Lebanon and in Iraq, the illegal detentions in Guantanamo Bay and 'extraordinary rendition' and the like.

The Ministry of Religious Affairs and Minorities is supposed to be an organisation that has the responsibility for protecting the minorities and promoting their welfare. Its main activity seems to be arranging pilgrimages for Muslims and non-Muslims of Pakistan. However, it also has to safeguard the rights of minorities as specified in the constitution of Pakistan. It has to protect the minorities from discrimination in all fields, and promote their welfare. The former minister in charge, Mr Derrick Cyprian, was from a religious minority. However, he resigned on the issue of separate electorates for religious minorities, a measure by Zia ul Haqq that Bishop Malik calls 'religious apartheid'. This measure by Zia ul Haqq effectively dismembered Pakistan into 5 states. Non-Muslims could vote only for a member of their own religious community, and Muslims could not vote for a candidate from a non-Muslim community. Since the vast number of the candidates by virtue of their preponderant majority have to be Muslim, this meant that Muslim Members of Parliament took no interest in the affairs and welfare of non-Muslim citizens. The Human Rights Monitor stated: 'The system of separate electorates is flawed, slanted, unjust and (an) inadequate mode of political participation. Besides infringing upon the right of (the) people of Pakistan to be equal citizens, this electoral system has practically disenfranchised the religious minorities of Pakistan'.[2] The present minister Zafarul

---

2   *Human Rights Monitor* (2000): 99.

Haqq is the son of Zia ul Haqq, the Martial Law Administrator mostly responsible for undermining the status of minorities in the country.

The Federal Advisory Council for Minority Affairs is also there. It comprises 65 members of the National Assembly and the four provincial assemblies,[3] including elected members and prominent members of the religious minorities. This council is supposed to make recommendations to the Government of Pakistan on matters of policy and other matters of concern to religious minorities.

In 1985 a non-lapsable fund for the welfare and upliftment of minorities had also been established with Rs 20 million set aside for this purpose, to be increased yearly. This amount is to provide financial assistance to individuals and families among the minorities in dire financial straits. It can also be used for developmental activities and acquisition of cemeteries.

In 1993 The National Commission for Minorities was also instituted for considering laws and executive procedures that may lead to discrimination and also to suggest remedial measures. It was also supposed to ensure that minorities participate fully and effectively in all aspects of life in Pakistan, and that minority religious buildings are preserved and maintained to be in good condition and functional.

These are very laudable aims and it is mystifying how in spite of all these measures the experience and prospects of religious minorities in Pakistan still remain bleak. Obviously, these measures are not being implemented effectively. Governmental commissions and Ministries might not be successful when the general attitude of the majority to minorities remains hostile and unsympathetic. The present disturbed state of affairs in the political scene and developments in world politics such as the situation in the Middle East may be to blame for some of the failures on the part of Governmental departments to carry out their responsibilities effectively. It is also to be suspected that a genuine will is lacking to make the best use of these resources to brighten the prospects of minorities. Government departments are notoriously bogged down in bureaucracy and may also be disadvantaged by corruption and inefficiency. It also has to be noted that since 1999 the Ministry of Religious Affairs has been combined with the Ministry of Culture and Sports. This move will inevitably lead to a lack of focus on minority issues. The ministry has therefore become more cumbersome and unable to pay adequate attention to its avowed objective of protecting and promoting the interests of the minorities.

Christian-Muslim dialogue

Bishop Malik told me that Christian-Muslim dialogue is a very hot subject. I should surmise that he meant by this that such dialogue is very vital and topical, something that people should pursue avidly. Bishop Malik said that dialogue is mainly on Christian initiative not so much Muslim. This might be a fact. Bishop Malik attributes this to the fact that Christians are in a minority in Pakistan and such dialogue is more to their interest than for the majority community. He opines that dialogue is necessary for peaceful coexistence and to remove misunderstanding

---

3   Panjab, Sindh, *Balochistan and North West Frontier Province.*

about each other's faith. He cited the instance of a textbook that describes Christians as believing in three Gods. These passages are written by Muslims who do not have an authentic understanding of Christianity. Bishop Malik has brought these errors to the notice of the authorities and would like either for descriptions of Christianity to be eliminated altogether from textbooks or written by Christian scholars.

The Christian Study Centre in Rawalpindi is an institution that is highly dialogue-oriented. It provides resources for the study of both Islam and Christianity and many Muslim as well as Christian scholars use it regularly. The Centre has facilities for scholars to reside and many Muslim Ulama stay there and carry out studies and research. It is obvious that this will create many a happy circumstance for engaging in Christian-Muslim dialogue. The Centre is an ecumenical venture initially started by the West Pakistan Council of Protestant Churches but later on joined by the Roman Catholic Church. Bishop Azariah is the present chair of the Centre and Dr Mehboob Sada its director. The Centre lists its objectives as:

1. To assist the Christian Churches in Pakistan in their attempt to gain a better understanding of their historical background, their existence as a part of the universal Church and of their particular calling in an Islamic state. Part of this work is to focus on the process of Islamicisation taking place in Pakistan and its impact on the position of women and minorities.
2. To undertake and encourage theological, academic and people-oriented research into the necessity and nature of Christian-Muslim relationships and the study of Islam.
3. To develop participatory studies and research which encourage dialogue, foster mutual understanding and promote cooperation in all essential spheres of life in Pakistan.
4. To stimulate evaluation, participation, study and research of Christian involvement in various spheres of nation building in Pakistan.[4]

Mrs Imtiaz, wife of Revd Imtiaz, Curate of the Church of Pakistan Cathedral in Lahore and an active church worker, told me she had participated in many inter-faith dialogue sessions. She had much criticism to voice about these meetings. She said that women found it difficult to participate in the interaction as they were often ignored by the males, not surprising in a patriarchal society such as Pakistan. About dialogue she offered the criticism that the sessions were not realistic. They tried to hide the realities and were constantly highlighting the commonalities as though there were no differences. In one session that she attended they were discussing the nature of God in Christianity and Islam. Mrs Imtiaz said that the God of Islam and the God of Christianity are not the same being. Christians say that God is love and Muslims say God is merciful but will not mention the love of God. They will also not depict God as a father. According to Mrs Imtiaz these are vital contrasts.

---

4   Moghal, Dominic, in *Churches' Commission on Mission Asia Forum Conference* (9th May 2003). *http://www.geocities.com/ccom_asia_forum/documents/030509_Asia_Day_ Conference_Moghal_paper.htm.*

This might be the reality but in dialogue there should be an element of compromise. In Islam the relationship between God and the human being is portrayed as that between a master and his servant. God is *Malik* and the human *abd*. Abd Allah (Servant of God) is a popular Muslim name for males. In Islam the majesty and power of God is highlighted rather than his love and fathership of the human. But these kinds of aspects of the divine nature are not entirely absent in Islam. God as creator is indeed a father figure in Islam also. And God's mercy and compassion are highlighted in the Basmalah[5] at the beginning of all Suras of the Qur'an.

Dialogue is however not aimed at syncretism but clearing misconceptions and arriving at an authentic 'insider view' of the other religion. Patient listening is the key to success in dialogue as also sensitivity and empathy. Differences need not be glossed over but there are always extenuating factors. For example, mercy is an attribute arising from love so the expressions 'God is love' and 'God is merciful' are not contradictory.

Some Muslims might view Christian initiatives at dialogue with suspicion. Butler and Chagathai state that sometimes it is rejected as a missionary device.[6] But of course the objective of dialogue is not religious conversion. They opine that such dialogue is rarely welcomed by Muslims as a new step towards forming better relationships, though some may pay lip-service to such initiatives.

Part of the problem is that the Christians, whose origins are mainly from the lowest echelons of society such as the Chuhras (sweepers), are looked down upon by the Muslim community. Ninety per cent of Christians are from a Dalit (untouchable caste) background. The remaining are Goans and Anglo-Indians and they are usually viewed as foreigners and not true Pakistanis.

Moreover, the depiction of Christians in Muslim writing is not generally approbative. I have already mentioned inauthentic and misconceived pronouncements in textbooks. Bishop Azariah said that in History books the emphasis is on the Crusades and the colonial era, both hardly conducive to bettering Christian-Muslim relations. A depiction of Islamic Spain or Muslims being given equal rights in modern European nations or the USA should be part of this discussion of Christian-Muslim relations. Iftikhar Malik writes:

> By reverting to a tunnel view of history, in an aura of exaggeration, the age-old religious tensions between Christianity and Islam are frequently cited to substantiate alarmist hypotheses of so-called clash of civilisations.[7]

It is extremely counterproductive to hearken back to these instances of confrontation between Christianity and Islam. Even President Bush has been guilty of this, though in his case it might have been a slip of the tongue. However, it reveals how deeply ingrained in Christian and Muslim psyche the Crusades are. As a matter of fact

---

5   *Bismillahi al Rahman al Rahim* (In the name of God, the Compassionate, the Merciful).

6   Butler, Robert A., and Chagathai, M. Ikram, *Trying to Respond* (Lahore, 1994), p. 326.

7   Malik, Ifthikar, *Islam, Nationalism and the West: Issues of Identity in Pakistan* (London, 1999), p. xvi.

the aetiology of the Crusades was very complex and was not simply a matter of Christian-Muslim antagonism. Moreover, it was the Seljuk Turks who ruled Palestine at that time, and not Arabs or other Muslims, and who prevented Christian pilgrims from visiting the Christian sacred sites such as the Holy Sepulchre. The Turks were as much hated by other Muslims as by the Christians and Jews of the region. As a matter of fact, one of the first actions of Salahuddin who recaptured Jerusalem from the Crusaders was to allow pilgrims to visit these places. Moreover, internal political, social and economic issues in Europe were also contributory factors as much as extraneous factors such as the inaccessibility of Christian sacred sites. It is also significant that some Crusaders attacked Jews and Byzantine Christians as well as Muslims.

But these can very well be the subject-matter of frank and sincere dialogue between Christians and Muslims and much misunderstanding and acrimony could be obviated by such discussions. But erroneous, insensitive, uninformed and unreflective depictions of these events in textbooks etc. can cause great harm. Christians have also been guilty of such stereotyped representations of Islam. Ifthikar Malik points out that even such intellectuals as Toynbee and James Joyce have been guilty of questioning Islam's relevance to human civilisation.[8]

Linda Walbridge points out that the dialogue is between highly educated Christian priests and very liberal Muslims.[9] This is not a good premise for genuine dialogue. Such dialogue should be between people of similar scholarly attainment in their religions and of commitment to their faith. Otherwise the dialogue will become purely perfunctory. Also it would be good for ordinary Muslims and Christians to meet and talk about their faith, not theologians only. However, Linda Walbridge notes that the interaction between Muslims and Christians has had a marked impact on the practice of Christianity in Pakistan: increased devotion and commitment to church attendance reflect the intensity with which Islam is practised in Pakistan.[10] Also a marked commitment to fasting in Lent and reverence bordering on the physical for the Bible, which is a notable phenomenon in Muslim attitudes to the Qur'an. For them the Qur'an is literally the word of God and part of His being and coeternal with Him. Therefore it is sacrosanct and treated very reverently. Removing shoes when entering the churches and segregation of men and women in the church might also be the result of emulating Muslims. Some Christians might even go to the extent of demanding a code of law similar to the Shari'ah. So they are drawn to the injunctions and stipulations of the Old Testament rather than to the New. It would almost seem to one that Islamic perspectives and attitudes have become normative for the Christians of Pakistan. Being the preponderant majority faith it seems that Christians would like to please the Muslims by trying to emulate their devotion to Islam and Islamic rituals. This is also a form of dialogue, a dialogue of emulation.

Christian-Muslim dialogue can also take the form of a dialogue of deeds. These are mutually beneficial actions by the two communities. Examples of this are not wanting in the Pakistan context. Co-operative efforts by Christians and Muslims in

---

8   Malik, p. 96.
9   Walbridge, Linda, *The Christians of Pakistan* (London, 2003), p. 187.
10 Ibid., p. 187.

social welfare activities and in sports activities such as at the YMCA (Young Men's Christian Association) are instances of this. The YMCA, though it is technically a Christian union, is patronised by Muslims and other faiths also as it provides a good venue for sports activities and indoor games and relaxing conversation among youth. Apparently some Christian clergy visit Muslim patients and it provides opportunities for positive interaction especially when Muslim patients would unburden their woes to a sincere and sympathetic Christian listener. The services of Christian nurses in hospitals and particularly hospices tending to dying Muslim patients have been particularly welcomed and even led to discussion of theological matters and social issues.[11] It is also worth noting that local believers, with the help of Christian organisations, were able to reach out to their Muslim neighbours in the aftermath of the October 2005 earthquake that killed 73,000 and injured 80,000 in the Kashmir area.[12]

It is said that for Bishop John Joseph, who became a martyr in the cause of the Blasphemy Law, dialogue took another form. It was a dialogue of social interaction between Christians and Muslims. Bishop John apparently had a lot of Muslim friends and his Punjabi Christian flock was proud of what he was doing to promote rapport between the two communities. He used to invite prominent Muslim citizens and officials and hold a dinner in his church. Undoubtedly this was a dialogue of social interaction, rather different from the intellectual dialogue of discussion and sharing of beliefs and ideology which happened elsewhere. On the other hand, some of the Catholic priests of Goan origin were critical of Bishop John's rather emotionally charged ways of approaching Christian-Muslim interaction and were of the opinion that he did not induce his flock to approach Muslims in the right ways, with sensitivity and respect.[13]

Christian schools are another venue for good interaction between Christians and Muslims. In reality the majority of students in these schools are Muslim, a reflection of the demographic situation in Pakistan. Christian schools have a good reputation for scholastic standards and are well favoured by parents keen on their wards getting a good education. Many told me that prominent leaders of Pakistan are graduates of such schools, for instance Benazir Bhutto and President Musharaff. Girls' schools run by Nuns are particularly noted for instilling good discipline and high academic standards in girls. Muslim parents favour such schools over co-educational ones, especially for older children. Chagathai opines that some Christians might think the Muslims are motivated only by pragmatic interests, such as a good education for their children. However, in my own experience I have found Muslims and others are highly appreciative of their time in Christian schools whatever the religious disparities might be. Amicable relationships have developed between individual students or teaching colleagues belonging to different faiths in such schools and it is a positive development which may even lead to doctrinal dialogue. Muslim students of Christian schools are prone to condemn violence against Christians.[14] A good

---

11 Butler and Chagathai, p. 329.
12 Reported in *Today's Christian* (January-February 2007).
13 Walbridge, p. 182.
14 Ibid.

example of dialogue of action comes from a Nun who headed a Christian college. She organised celebration of Milad un Nabi (Birthday of the Prophet) in the college. This was a most commendable initiative, considering the high esteem in which the Prophet is held in Islam. Undoubtedly the Nun's action was greatly appreciated by Muslim students and their parents. Joint celebration of religious festivals is a preferred form of dialogue of deeds. This can include rights of passage ceremonies such as birthdays, circumcision, and marriages. Many Muslims invite Christians to these functions and *vice versa*. I myself have attended many Muslim rites of passage ceremonies. Moreover, this can be a stepping stone to more participatory religious activities such as common worship tried out by the Anglican Church in Britain several times. Gandhi, the Mahatma, favoured such common prayer meetings and held them frequently in his ashram and in Delhi, though it could not have pleased fundamentalists. As matter of fact he was assassinated by a Hindu fanatic on his way to such a meeting on 30 January 1948.

However, criticism of Christian schools is also voiced. They were in colonial times agencies for evangelisation and proselytisation and carried a stigma for Muslims. They hardly engage in such things any more, at least overtly. Missionary schools and colleges are popular and in demand, yet some Muslims still see them as agents of Westernisation preventing their wards from becoming loyal to Pakistan and Islam. Butler and Chagathai state that they are seen as 'hotbeds of alien ideology'.[15] Moreover, there is the criticism that they cater mainly to the middle and upper middle classes only as they charge fees, unlike the state-run schools, a fact commented upon to me by the Sub-Editor of *The Dawn* whom I interviewed. However, standards in state-run schools and private madrassas can be appalling and therefore parents who could afford the expense would like to send their children to Christian schools whatever their perception of the problems of a 'hidden curriculum' might be.

Christian-Muslim relations are said to be best in Karachi. Karachi is a cosmopolitan city being a port, and thus exposed more to foreign influences and therefore more receptive to such influences and less exclusive-minded than cities farther inland. The presence of sailors and visitors from other countries with them is certain to broaden one's perspective and thus should provide opportunities for interaction and communication between people of different faiths and cultures. Butler and Chagathai state that there the Ulama are not so well favoured as in other cities and in rural inland regions of Pakistan.[16] They mention that contacts are best at the lower middle class level and among working class people.

Interaction between teachers and students and teaching colleagues are also opportunities for dialogue. Butler and Chagathai state that Muslims in Christian educational institutions are prone to stress the nearness of the two religions and also decry that Pakistan is not conforming to Islamic ideals of tolerance to other faiths.[17] This is among a highly educated class, so discussions should be at a more sophisticated level and will tackle issues in depth rather than on a casual or superficial level. People co-operating in social welfare activities such as tending to the sick and

---

15 Butler and Chagathai, p. 25.
16 Ibid., p. 28.
17 Ibid.

the poor, or tending to the dying have very good opportunities for sharing ideas and for cultivating mutual empathy. The Guidelines for Inter-Faith Dialogue published by the British Council of Churches define one of the objectives of dialogue as:

'To bring common insights as well as distinctive insights to discussion of social, educational, healthcare and ecological issues ... to work together for world peace and disarmament ...'[18] It is seen that Muslims engaging in dialogue or studying in Christian institutions are quick to condemn violence against Christians.

On a negative note some Christians might think that Muslim concern for them could be pragmatic or motivated by material benefits such as a good education. Also some Christians would wish to be seen as different from Muslim citizens – this is not a positive circumstance for national unity and integration. There is no harm in trying to be a better citizen and individual, to have better morals, ethics and values, but this should not lead to a feeling of superiority for Muslims or Christians. When national identity can transcend feelings of religious identity real dialogue and integration will take place. You cannot enter into dialogue with a superiority complex.

The Christian Study Centre in Rawalpindi, which, as I have mentioned earlier, is an institution oriented towards Christian-Muslim dialogue, maintains contacts with Muslim scholars in the Islamic Research institute, Islamabad. It is salutary that articles touching on each other's religion are exchanged for scrutiny and comment before being published. This will obviate any material prejudicial to each other's faith and also misrepresentations. The Christian Study Centre also engages in lecturing and teaching and is ready to teach Islamic Studies to Christians with emphasis on dialogue with Muslims. It is also ready to teach about the Christian faith to Muslims if called upon to do so. Mutual authentic understanding and knowledge of each other's faith obviously will go a long way to establishing rapport, and eradicate misconceptions and stereotyping of each other's religion which lie at the heart of much inter-religious conflict or are used by fanatics to fan the flames of mistrust and hostility.

Loyola Hall, founded in 1962 by the late Swiss Jesuit priest Robert Butler, is another institution which is a meeting point for Christian and Muslim minds. It has a fine research library and functions in the same style as the Christian Study Centre. It holds regular meetings of a Christian and Muslim scholarly discussion group where subjects chosen by the members are discussed. This is especially significant for Lahore, which, though the cultural capital of Pakistan is also a hotbed of Islamic politics. However, *The Christian Voice* reports many events in Lahore that presage good relations between the two faiths. For instance, Christians attended a conference hosted by the Badshahi Mosque.[19] This seventeenth-century mosque constructed during Mughal times has one of the largest courtyards of any mosque, capable of holding one hundred thousand worshippers at one time. The Imam of the mosque, Maulana Kabir Azad, revealed himself to be an enlightened and tolerant Muslim leader by inviting Christians into his mosque. In his address he quoted the famous

---

18 The British Council of Churches, *Relations with People of Other Faiths – Guidelines for Dialogue in Britain* (London, 1983), p. 6.

19 *The Christian Voice* (25.1.2004): 7.

statement of Jesus in the Sermon on the Mount: 'Blessed are the peace makers – for they shall see God' (Matthew 5:9).[20] On another occasion, lighting a peace candle on Easter Day, he is said to have remarked that 'We are ready to spread the message of peace and harmony as preached by Jesus.'[21] Clearly there are Muslim leaders also who take the initiative for bettering Christian-Muslim relations in Pakistan. Similarly, the Markaze Bilal Mosque welcomed a Christian delegation to the mosque on 15 August 2004, National Independence Day.[22] *The Christian Voice* reports that on 28 March 2004 a church centre led a rally against the occupation of Iraq by Western forces.[23] The NCID (National Commission for Inter-religious Dialogue) is reported to have organised a walk and rally for peace in Lahore on 29 August 2004 in which Christian, Muslim, Hindu and Sikh leaders participated. Slogans such as 'Long live Pakistan' were shouted and in front of the Lahore Press Club multi-faith prayers for Pakistan were made in the worship style of each religion.[24]

Butler and Chagathai mention a Christian missionary who runs a correspondence course, which is taken up by 6000 students.[25] This is indeed surprising in a milieu such as that of Pakistan. This reveals that the Muslims of Pakistan are not innately averse to finding out about other faiths. Even more amazing is the information that some of these students have become converts to Christianity. This must run counter to the official policy, but the web is a system which is very difficult to censor and control, so it is quite feasible that Christian evangelisation that is not possible openly can be done on the worldwide internet. However, though evangelisation and conversion are not primary purposes of dialogue, a device by which people could study and understand each other's faith is salutary and helpful in removing misconceptions, engendering empathy and promoting religious tolerance.

Bishop Samuel Azariah, Bishop of Raiwind Diocese of the Church of Pakistan, admits that the Christians of Pakistan find themselves in a unique socio-political situation. That the substantial part of the church is due to conversion by Missionary organisations that operated, though not under the aegis of the colonial administration, but at least with its tacit approval, has painted an image that the Christians of Pakistan are the toadies and stool-pigeons of the Christian West. The Bishop also undoubtedly refers to their origins from the lowest social classes. Thus, Bishop Azariah states that they experience a backlash when the wars in Afghanistan and Iraq led by the West began and when traumatic incidents against Palestinians happen in the West Bank and Gaza.

The Bishop is, however, optimistic that efforts by the Christian community of Pakistan at dialogue with Muslims can counter these negative images. Such dialogue is still viewed with suspicion by Muslims, but on the other hand much progress has

---

20 Ibid.
21 *The Christian Voice* (8 April 2004).
22 *The Christian Voice* (15 August 2004): 6.
23 *The Christian Voice* (28 March 2004).
24 *The Christian Voice* (22 August 2004).
25 Butler and Chagathai, p. 330.

been made considering that a few years ago Christian-Muslim dialogue was not considered, the Bishop states, a very bright possibility.[26]

The NCIDE (National Commission for Inter-Religious Dialogue and Ecumenism) is an organisation (founded in 1965) through which Christian and Muslim leaders have jointly condemned attacks on Christian churches by Muslim militants. The NCIDE is the organisation that greeted Muslims on Id al Adha. The Heralds of Peace is another Pakistani organisation that promotes Christian-Muslim dialogue.

The objectives of the NCIDE are as follows: to work for peace and reconciliation in Pakistan. Their vision is to ensure equality, peaceful co-existence and harmony among all ethnic and religious groups in Pakistan. They have set up projects such as a peace and education programme for children, joint celebration of religious festivals of all major faiths, peace prayers and rallies at regular intervals, and ongoing dialogue and cooperation at every rung of society. They aspire to initiate value education, and bring out a publication to create awareness of their objectives, especially among the youth.[27] Bishop Andrew Francis, Catholic Bishop of Multan, is the chair of NCIDE. Bishop Francis recently spoke out against the stereotype of Christians of Pakistan favouring the West. He stated categorically that the Christians look for leadership only to the President and Prime Minister of Pakistan, not to the US or any other Western nation.[28] Thus he tried to allay Muslim fears of extra-territorial loyalty of the Christians of Pakistan. Beginning on 11 December 2005 it held a four-day seminar on inter-religious dialogue in Lahore attended among others by the Vatican's Chair of Inter-religious Dialogue Commission, Monsignor Michael L. Douglas, and Senator Muhammad Ali Durrani, an advisor to President Musharaff. The senator stated that both the President and Prime Minister Shaukat Ali were in favour of inter-religious dialogue.[29] It has also to be noted that Pakistan was joint sponsor at the United Nations with the Philippines of the resolution on Promotion of Inter-Religious and Inter-Cultural Dialogue, Understanding and Cooperation for Peace.

The Human Development Centre established in 1985 is another organisation that promotes communal harmony and particularly Christian-Muslim dialogue in Pakistan. It has formed local peace committees that seek to improve community relations and try to mediate in disputes between Christians and Muslims. For example, when a Christian girl was kidnapped in Dawakhri, a not uncommon occurrence, the local peace committee mediated and brought the matter to a peaceful and just conclusion, though at the beginning the family of the girl threatened violence against the kidnappers.[30] It seems that when the Peace Committee was first formed Muslims and Christians did not want to sit together and discuss issues. Gradually there was a thaw when the local leadership was motivated through seminars and

---

26 Qayyum, Naveen, 'Minorities and dialogue: a sense of shared vulnerability', in *World Council of Churches* (13 June 2005).

27 See website http://isf2006.wsfindia.org/organisation_profile_forlist.php?orgains_id=2204.

28 *The Christian Voice* (1 February 2004).

29 Reported in *Asia Media* (11 December 2005).

30 See conflict resolution case in HDC website http://hdcpakistan.tripod.com/id2.html.

such public awareness programmes, and the Christians invited the Muslims to meet them at their church. Afterwards the Muslims in turn invited them to meet together at a mosque. There are women's branches also for these peace committees. Women stage interactive theatre to get the message of peace and reconciliation across. Such dramatisation and role-playing are effective tools for influencing communities to seek greater harmony and avail of the benefits that accrue from communal co-operation and peace.

The Pakistan Association for Inter-Religious Dialogue is another body that has played an effective role in bring Christians and Muslims together in Pakistan. It has been successful in promoting opposition to the system of separate electorates for religious communities and for identifying religion in individual passports.

Naveen Qayyum, from Pakistan, a cinematographer working with the World Council of Churches has produced a documentary titled *Building Bridges* which has taken as a case study the context of Christians living in Muslim majority Pakistan. The film is said to highlight the complexities of ecumenical dialogue.

Another Roman Catholic body is the National Commission for Justice and Peace. This organisation was formed by the Pakistan Catholic Bishops' Conference of Pakistan in 1985. It has five regional offices (Rawalpindi, Gujranwala, Faisalabad, Multan and Hyderabad) and its head office in Lahore. It provides legal aid and human rights education. Under the legal aid programme, the Commission provides services including legal counselling and financial assistance. So far the Commission has dealt with about 600 cases during the last 18 years.[31]

This organisation has brought the plight of minorities in Pakistan to the attention of international agencies such as the United Nations. In a letter to the Working Group on Minorities of the UN High Commission on Human Rights they have invited the attention of the international community to religious intolerance and lack of religious freedom in Pakistan. They recommended a six-point programme to the Government of Pakistan to redress these issues:

1. To set up an independent permanent commission for minorities with powers of a tribunal, which can entertain complaints and provide redress on urgent basis.

2. To implement the recommendations given by UN Special Rapporteur on Religious Tolerance after his visit to Pakistan in 1996 that it should repeal all the discriminatory laws and policies including Blasphemy Laws, Hudood Ordinance, Law of Evidence etc without any delay.

3. To take serious measures to ensure that minorities can participate in economic and public life without discrimination, including monitoring of recruitment practices. Laws should be passed and enforced to criminalise hate speech in any form, and;

4. To sign and ratify the important UN treaties such as ICCPR (International Covenant on Civil and Political Rights), ICESCR (International Covenant on

---

31 Pax Christi International website: http://www.paxchristi.net/members/html/asia_pacific_overview.php?mo_id=45&mo_name=National%20Commission%20for%20Justice%20and%20Peace%20of%20Pakistan.

Economic, Social and Cultural Rights), CAT (Committee Against Torture) and should make arrangements in the country for educating masses on their rights and responsibilities under these treaties.

5. They also called upon the United Nations to ensure the follow-up visit of UN Special Rapporteur on Religious Tolerance to Pakistan as soon as possible to assess the situation, ascertain causes of religious discrimination, implement religious tolerance and to give recommendations to the UNCHR and the government of Pakistan.

6. They also suggested to the Working Group to recommend the appointment of a Special Representative of the Secretary General on minorities.

The general atmosphere in inter-religious relations in Pakistan is not conducive to inter-faith dialogue. The wars in Afghanistan and Iraq, especially the latter, have vitiated relations between the Muslim world and the West, and have given added momentum to the ascendancy of Islamic fundamentalism and militancy. Political parties based on Islamist ideology have gained ground in recent times. But there are many Muslims in Pakistan who are of a tolerant and liberal attitude to other religions. In fact the majority of the intellectuals and educated sections are of this ilk. However, the Muslim masses are easily persuaded that the Christian West is on a collision course with Islam and is out to destroy the religion. This does not make for a good premise to improving relations of Islam with other faiths in a Muslim majority nation. Muslims are angry with the West and see shades of the colonial era in the occupation of Afghanistan and Iraq by USA and the British and a few other Western forces. There is also the Kashmir issue and consequent souring of relations with Hindu India. In this climate it is a difficult task to foster good inter-faith relations and persuade Muslims to engage in inter-faith dialogue.

In spite of this climate adverse to inter-faith dialogue there are many measures that the Christian community of Pakistan are taking to foster good Christian-Muslim relations and promote Christian-Muslim dialogue. Such moves from a beleaguered community are admirable and worthy of support. Far-sighted Christian leaders have instituted organisations for this purpose and they are now well established and doing good work, albeit in a political climate not conducive to success in the work of rapprochement between the two communities. Several enlightened Muslim leaders are also responsive to such initiatives. Moreover, at an ordinary level dialogue of good deeds, service and the opportunities of living and working in close proximity are bringing together Christians and Muslims and leading to the cultivation of informal friendships and even theological discussion. The Government of Pakistan is generally supportive of such initiatives though they could do much more, not the least by repealing the unworkable and misused Blasphemy Law.

International organisations also help in supporting Christian-Muslim dialogue in Pakistan. The Vatican, the Church of England (through NIFCON, (Network for Inter-Faith Concerns in the Anglican Communion), the World Council of Churches and such international Christian organisations have supported and aided dialogue. Archbishop Rowan Williams, Head of the Anglican Communion, in a recent visit to Pakistan met Muslim religious leaders and intellectuals and visited a Muslim Madrassa. He also lectured at the Islamic University, Islamabad. The visit shows considerable initiative by the Church of Pakistan in augmenting good Christian-Muslim relations, and the reciprocity of Muslims at a high level to such initiatives is encouraging. The World Council of Churches in 2002 sent an ecumenical delegation to study the inter-faith situation in Pakistan. Amnesty International and the Human Rights wing of the United Nations have also been supportive of dialogue-oriented organisations in Pakistan and intercede frequently on behalf of persecuted Christians in individual cases as well as general issues such as the Blasphemy Law. Amendments to the Hudood laws passed recently in the Women's Protection Bill[32] of November 2006, though they do not go far enough, are most probably the result of such pressure on the Government of Pakistan by international agencies.

It is to be hoped that when the problems in Afghanistan and the Middle East are resolved in a just and lasting manner, the political atmosphere in Pakistan will become stable, and then these efforts at Christian-Muslim dialogue will bear greater fruit, and lead to very good relations between the two communities and the eradication of violence, persecution and discrimination.

---

32 Rape is now to be tried only by secular courts, not Shari'a courts as formerly. Often the victim had to produce four male witnesses to rape, a near impossibility, or be accused of adultery herself, which is punishable by death.

Chapter Eight

Conclusion

The state of Christian-Muslim relations in Pakistan seems to present a bleak picture. Pakistan started out with a fair and just constitution that matched the aspirations of its founders Muhammad Ali Jinnah and Allama Iqbal. They were people of towering intellect, wide experience of politics and enlightened vision. Though Pakistan was created to be a homeland for Muslims it was not conceived as an Islamic state. It was modelled on secular ideals much as most of the states in the West. The religious neutrality and equality of the Pakistan constitution has however considerably eroded as time went on. It is a young nation as far as its individual history is concerned – sixty years is infinitesimal in comparison to the history of the Indian subcontinent, though such a history is relevant to Pakistan also – continuity with its pre-1947 past cannot be avoided. However, within these sixty years, in comparison to its counterpart and neighbour and in some senses arch rival India, changes in Pakistan have been much more eventful. It has not presented a picture of stability. Part of this is due to its location. Many parts of the Pakistan region of the subcontinent had not been so tightly governed by the colonial regime as the other parts. The British did not try to Westernise or impose their own brand of ethics and political configurations on this region as much as they did in the plains and the central parts of India. Rai Shakil Akhatar mentions that being the frontiers of the Empire the British Government of India did not uproot the tribal, feudal and traditional ways of the Pakistan region. Moreover, they came under direct colonial rule much later than other central regions of India.[1] So the culture, the political system and the general ethos of the Pakistan region are more indigenous and tribal than in the rest of India. It is a frontier region and subject to many influences from outside in comparison to peninsular India.

World events and the ambiguous foreign policy of the United States and Britain have adversely affected inter-religious relations in Pakistan. A substantial section of the populace of Pakistan is educated, intelligent, moderate, tolerant to other faiths and cultures, reasonable and progressive-minded. In my conversations with Muslim educators, journalists and intellectuals I observed that they were marked by all these qualities. But this what I may call the silent majority find it difficult to support the policies of the United States and its proposed war on terror. There are no doubt considerable numbers of jihadis, fundamentalists, militants and extremists in Pakistan. It has been a hotbed of politics and these groups have particularly been spawned by Pakistan's long-standing dispute with India over Kashmir, and the conflicts in Afghanistan. Thus the geographical location of this nation has also been conducive to the formation of militant groups. Moreover, the Wahabi ideology spread by oil

---

1   Akhatar, Rai Shakil, *Media, Religion and Politics in Pakistan* (Oxford, 2000), p. 215.

wealth from its headquarters, Saudi Arabia, is very strong in Pakistan. Wahabism, which is somewhat analogous to the Protestant Reformation in Christianity, sought to purify Islam from its accretions from other cultures and faiths, which are looked upon by this puritanical form of Islam as *bida* (innovation) or *kufra* (atheism) or even as *shirk* (polytheism), the unforgiveable sin in Islam. It is particularly against Sufism, the spiritual, contemplative and other-worldly and mystical form of Islam which was to a great extent responsible for the spread of Islam in this region in the first place, owing to its tolerance, adaptability and readiness to absorb from other cultures and even other faiths. Wahabism by itself is not a dangerous ideology but it has the potential to breed fanaticism and extremism. The Islamic political parties in Pakistan subscribe to this form of Islam and world events have strengthened their hands. The moderate majority is therefore silent and does not exert much effort to oppose this radicalism. The Palestinian issue is also a vital factor in the breeding of Muslim *angst* and frustration, which is reflected in the apparent ascendancy of militant groups among Pakistani Muslims. The regime of Zia ul Haqq no doubt gave a tremendous fillip to these trends and to a great extent fused these radical elements into the body politic and higher echelons of the government.

The Christians of Pakistan are truly Pakistanis and they were there from time immemorial. As a matter of fact, if we believe the evidence some of which I have discussed in Chapter 2 they were there well before the advent of Islam. Culturally and linguistically, and except for the matter of their faith in all ways, they are indigenous Pakistanis. They are little different from the Muslim Pakistanis in many aspects of life, and even in their names. But constitutional and political developments in Pakistan have militated against their feeling of belonging to the nation and they can very well feel marginalised and alienated from mainstream Pakistani life. This is a great shame. They are a struggling community, since many of them have their origins in the lower echelons of Pakistani society such as the Chuhras. However, the Christians run the best educational institutions in Pakistan and they have the potential to come up through education and hard work if they are accorded equal opportunities in employment and in economic enterprise. Even as early as in 1953 Justice Cornelius, a Catholic and Chief Justice of the Pakistan Supreme Court from 1960 to 1968, had warned against 'A general feeling of despair, a widespread lack of confidence and a common readiness to anticipate the worst'.[2] But the problems that the Christian community face in modern-day Pakistan may quite well engender such a feeling.

Even if Pakistan did eventually become an Islamic state, which is what the present trends point to, the situation of non-Muslims there should not be compromised. There are many passages in the Qur'an and the Hadith which enjoin Muslims to treat non-Muslims fairly and with dignity and honour. These relate not only to freedom of worship but also all other rights and obligations relating to social life and the rights of citizens.[3] The Prophet has been reported to have stated that he will oppose

---

    2   Quoted in Butler, R.A. and Chagathai, M.I., *Trying to Respond* (Lahore, 1994), p. 336. Justice Alvin Robert Cornelius was Chief Justice of the Pakistan Supreme Court from 1960 to 1968.

    3   See, Doi, A Rahman I, *Non-Muslims Under Shari'ah* (Lahore, 1981), p. 29.

in litigation any one who oppresses a non-Muslim or taxes him beyond his capacity.[4] The Qur'an specifically enjoins Muslims to do justice to even those they hate or those who hate the Muslims.[5]

In this light what is happening in Pakistan is extremely un-Islamic. For the constitutional amendments have gradually eroded equality of minorities before the law, and draconian laws such as the Blasphemy Law have made a mockery of this injunction not to be oppressive of the minorities. In Chapter 5 I have given numerous examples of how the law has been misused to settle personal grudges, property disputes and as expression of fanaticism. Extra-judicial killings by extremist vigilantes such as the Sipahi-I-Sahaba have made a travesty of the legal process. The police are not making sincere efforts to apprehend these killers. The fact that many of these offences are non-bailable has meant Christians and others have been incarcerated in prison over long periods before a final verdict is pronounced. In some cases Christian detainees have been murdered in prison. Others languishing in jail have not been permitted visitors, a point that the Human Rights Commission has pointed out in their appeal to the Government. False accusations of blasphemy have also meant that the victims and their families are subject to social ostracism and even death threats by militant Muslims. The Pakistan Human Rights Commission led by Magsaysay Award winner I.A. Rahim has been eloquent against these miscarriages of justice, and has called for a moratorium on carrying out the death penalty, and eventually, in line with the practice in many developed nations, a total ban on the death penalty. They have pointed out the weaknesses in the legal processes of Pakistan, corruption in the police, and alleged biases against women and the religious minorities. Obviously, many of these convictions leading to the death penalty are unsafe. While progressive nations are either banning the death penalty or reducing the contingencies under which it can be awarded, under Zia's regime (1977-1988) many were added, such as blasphemy against the Prophet, so that at present there are 27 crimes under which the death penalty can be imposed, whereas earlier capital punishment was only liable for murder and treason.[6] The *quisas* and *diyat* provision in the penal code whereby a murderer can go free if the victim's family accepts financial compensation is an anachronism and not compatible with values of a modern state.

It is clear that the Christians of Pakistan acknowledge that Islam is the majority religion of Pakistan and they are not wholly averse to being in an Islamic state. The problem is in how such a state is defined. If it is defined in a classical sense by which the Christians and other religious minorities become *ahl al Dhimma* and have to pay *jizya* (poll tax) or *kharaj* (land tax) then they are not in favour of that. The question of payment of Jizya by religious minorities has been raised now and then in Pakistan, once even by a Minister of Religious Affairs.[7] This is because they did not become subject to the state of Pakistan by virtue of being conquered or even by immigration. They just happened to be in that part of British India that became Pakistan. They can

---

4   Ibid., p. 37.

5   Surat al Maidah, v. 9.

6   See Ebrahim Zofeen, 'Death Penalty – Pakistan', in *Inter-Press Service News Agency* (14 February 2007).

7   Butler and Chagathai, p. 344.

at the most be looked upon as people of treaty or *ahl al Ahd (people of truce)*. In an Islamic state which for the Christians is *Dar al Suhl (land of agreement)* treaties have to be honoured and so people such as Christians have to be treated as equal citizens of the Islamic state and can be adjudged to possess an Islamic nationality (*al jiziyyah al Islamiyya*).[8] This may be why Justice Cornelius remarked 'I am a constitutional Muslim'.[9] Tarik Jan argues that the tension between the law and the individual or 'the never-ending conflict between the societal good and the individual rights, so often the case in secular societies', is mostly non-existent in an Islamic state.[10] However, this is not borne out by a close reading of the issues of individual rights and the rights of religious minorities in the Shari'a. Also according to the Shari'a they have perfect freedom to practise and profess their faith that includes the right to propagate their religion. They also have freedom of expressing their views orally and in writing, even those that are critical of Islam.[11] Christians are well aware of course that the right to propagate religion has to be exercised discreetly in Pakistan. Christian celebrations and processions are conducted by them only in the vicinity of the churches so as not to inflame the feelings of extremist Muslims.

It is however a fact that many Christians think Muslims in Pakistan look upon religious minorities as second class citizens, a circumstance that might lead to discrimination in the matter of education and employment.[12] They are not adequately represented in the legislature, there are no Christians in the Senate, for example, and not many in the police and the armed services. In any justly constituted nation there is a need for empowerment of the minorities to ensure their well-being. A retired Christian soldier told me that no Christian can now expect to be recruited to the armed forces. In Chapter 4 I have documented many of the problems suffered by Christians in Pakistani society such as aggression by Muslim fundamentalists, problems in education, in the legal sphere and in the religious domain. In a democracy the safety and preservation and implementation of the rights of the minorities become the responsibility of the majority since the government and administration of the state are mainly in their hands. Thus it is unto the majority community to safeguard the constitutional provisions and human rights prerogatives of minorities such as the Christians. The constitution of Medina and the example set by the Prophet demonstrate that Islam has always favoured multi-confessionalism. In Medina, the first Islamic state, there were Jews, Christians, polytheists and even atheists, but the rights, safety and interests of all were safeguarded in the Constitution of Medina. The clause: 'The Jews of al-Aus, their freedmen and themselves have the same standing with the people of this document in purely loyalty from the people of this document. Loyalty is a protection against treachery'. in the Constitution of Medina also indicates that non-Muslims were accorded equal status with Muslims in Medina

---

8   Doi, p. 22.

9   Quoted in Butler and Chagathai, p. 349.

10   Jan, Tarik, 'Questioning the Blasphemy Laws, a discussion', in Tarik Jan (ed.) *Pakistan between Secularism and Islam: Ideology, Power and Conflict* (Islamabad, 1998), pp. 241-56, p. 245.

11   Butler and Chagathai, p. 340.

12   Mentioned in ibid., p. 345.

and in return the constitution demanded their loyalty and avoidance of betraying the state. As I have said before there is no evidence that Christians have been or wish to be disloyal to Pakistan. If they are in favour of disestablishing the state it is because the majority faith has not helped them, and has not acted fairly towards them.

So even when the Government is tied down to a particular majority faith the interests of other faith communities need not be militated against provided that the state religion does not misuse its dominant position and seeks to help the minority religions. This is what the Muslims of Pakistan have to do. The Christians on their part have to get rid of the stigma of their association with British colonialism, an association engendered by the fact of the collaboration between Western Christian missions and the British regime of India. The present generation of Christians however are innocent of what has happened more than 60 years ago, and has nothing to do with their origins as converts from Hindu and Muslim communities in British India and are thoroughly rooted in Pakistani life. They are also making determined efforts to indigenise worship in the churches so that Christianity can be seen to be a religion of the native soil rather than a religion of the West. However, the stigma persists in Muslim minds and often identifies them with the actions of the USA and the United Kingdom, a most unfortunate circumstance for their relations with the Muslims in the present disturbed context of Islam-West relations. Sensible Muslims can however acknowledge that the link between the Christians of Pakistan and the West is mythical and has no basis in fact.

The question of loyalty to the state is of paramount importance to any community. If the Muslims of Pakistan suspect that the Christians are disloyal to the nation, then their perspective of Christians is going to be a perennially blighted one. Christians have done nothing to merit such an evaluation. But, as Joshua Fazl-ud-din comments, even honest differences of opinion may be mistaken for disloyalty and treachery and dealt with in a heavy-handed manner by Muslims.[13] This is also the result of national identity coalescing with an Islamic identity, excluding non-Muslims from being real citizens, and bringing all of them into the category of aliens to the nation state. Terms such as 'spies', 'enemies', 'kaffirs' and 'unsympathetic to the national cause' can be used by some Muslims to describe Christians. This is why in religiously plural states a secularly constituted nation is best. Thus many Christians are in favour of Pakistan abandoning the notion of an Islamic state. Zia ul Haqq tried to create a state within the state by forming separate electorates. The Christians fought this tooth and nail and the project was abandoned.

It is a hopeful sign that even in the midst of this vitiated circumstance of inter-faith relations there have been efforts at Christian-Muslim dialogue and improvement of Inter-faith relations. In Chapter 7 I have outlined some of the institutions, projects and initiatives in this direction. Some of these such as the Ministry of Religious Affairs and Minorities and the National Commission for Minorities are government-sponsored and religiously neutral inter-faith projects. Many of them are Christian initiatives. The Christian Study Centre in Rawalpindi, Loyola Hall in Lahore and the National Commission for Inter-Religious Dialogue and Ecumenism (NCIDE) are prominent examples. Their work is no doubt bearing some fruit, though they still

---

13 Fazl-ud-din, Joshua, *The Future of Christians in Pakistan* (Lahore, 1949), p. 44.

have a long way to go in realising their ideals and achieving the objective of stable and harmonious inter-faith relations in Pakistan. The Human Rights Commission of Pakistan and Human Development Centre and such voluntary organisations have also a significant role to play in this. International bodies such as the United Nations Human Rights Commission and Amnesty International are also campaigning for inter-communal harmony and justice in Pakistan.

President Pervez Musharaff has been extremely supportive of Christians and the rights and protection of minorities. He shows considerable enlightenment and moderation in his statements. His polices are in a sense offsetting the prejudiced and biased actions of another ruler who came to power through a coup, Zia ul Haqq. *The Christian Voice* reports that he stated that as Muslims they shared the joys of Christmas with the Christians.[14] He has also hailed efforts for inter-faith harmony. In an article he has called for enlightened moderation by Muslims and asked them to shun the path of extremism.[15] Father James Channan, Chair of the United Religions Initiative, is of the view that the present Pakistan administration seeks to assure equal respect for all citizens and promote inter-faith harmony and peace.[16] Musharaff, though he initially came to power through a *coup d'état*, has proved himself to be tackling the issue of inter-faith relations with more acumen and discernment than many former elected rulers.

But Musharaff's hands are to some extent tied in view of the current political exigencies of Pakistan. He cannot totally alienate the Muttahida Majlis Amal and such fundamentalistic Muslim organisations. He seems to be waiting for the right opportunity and circumstances so that he can avoid disruption of political stability to revise and rectify or maybe even repeal legislations such as the draconian Hudood Laws and Blasphemy Laws. He is walking a tightrope, a balancing act between his aspirations for justice and human rights for the religious minorities, and incurring the wrath of the Muslim fundamentalists of Pakistan who are now in the ascendancy in Pakistan, mainly due to the erroneous foreign policies of USA and its allies. The 'war on terror' that President Bush has initiated and of which President Musharaff is an ally has not helped matters. There is little support for the American policies in Pakistan and much anger against the suffering of the people of Iraq, Afghanistan and Palestine. In this context there is not much that President Musharaff can do to set right the anomalies, abuses and injustices that laws like the Blasphemy Law engender in Pakistan.

One can however be sanguine about the future of Christian-Muslim relations in Pakistan. Pakistan has considerable numbers of highly educated, intelligent, moderate and broad-minded Muslims. The Christian community is trying hard to reach out to the Muslims and form good relations with them. Pakistan has done well in the scientific field and has the potential and resources to become an economic power in South Asia. With better economic prosperity for the masses and with greater political stability inter-faith relations in Pakistan are bound to improve. A requirement will be

---

14 *The Christian Voice* (4 January 2004).

15 Musharaff, Pervez, 'Time for enlightened moderation', in *Dawa'h Highlights*, XV/ 5 (May-June 2004): 5-8, 6.

16 Reported in *The Christian Voice* (11 July 2004).

political settlement and stability in Palestine, Afghanistan and Iraq and in Pakistan's relations with India. If that happens, the fundamentalists, extremists and militants will be marginalised and Pakistan will present a more politically stable scene than it evinces now. The voice of the moderate majority, now silent, will again be heard. That will be extremely conducive to good inter-faith relations there.

Bibliography

Primary sources

Interviews

Bishop Alexander John Malik, Moderator for the Church of Pakistan
Bishop Samuel Azariah, Bishop of Raiwind Diocese, Church of Pakistan
Professor Razul Baksh, Head of Social Sciences, Lahore University of Management
 Sciences
Dr Raziya Sultana, Department of History, Quaid I Azam University, Islamabad
Mr Imran Khan, Leader of Tareekh I Insaaf
Sub-Editor, *The Dawn*, Lahore
Mrs Imtiaz, Lahore Cathedral

Journals

The Christian Voice
Al Mushir
Dawa'h Highlights
Friday Times, 3-9 September 2004
The Times, 11 May 1998
Justice and Peace Commission Report, 18 July 2004
AsiaNews.It, 29 May 2006
Universe, Catholic Newspaper, 3 July 2006
Pakistan Christian Post, 30 May 2006
Human Rights Watch Publications, vol. 5, no. 13, 19 September 1993, 'Persecuted
 Minorities and Writers in Pakistan'
Pakistan Link News, 27 April 2006
IFEX International Freedom of Expression Exchange, 12 March 2002
Today's Christian, January-February 2007
Qayyum, Naveen, 'Minorities and dialogue: a sense of shared vulnerability', *World
 Council of Churches*, 13 June 2005
Asia Media, 11 December 2005
Human Rights Monitor, 2000
Today's Christian, January-February 2007

Secondary sources

Abbas, Hassan, *Pakistan's Drift into Extremism* (New York: East Gate Books, 2005).

Ahmad, Mumtaz, 'Revivalism, Islamisation, sectarianism and violence in Pakistan', in Baxter, C. and Ahmed, Khaled (eds), *Pakistan, The State in Crisis* (Lahore: Vanguard Books, 2002).

Ahmad, Mumtaz, 'Revivalism, Islamisation, sectarianism and violence in Pakistan', in Bootes, Craig, and Akhtar, Rai Shakil (eds), *Media, Religion and Politics in Pakistan* (Oxford: Oxford University Press, 2000), pp. 101-21.

Alawi, Hamza, 'Ethnicity, Muslim Society and the Pakistan Ideology', in Weiss, Anita, M. (ed.) *Islamic Reassertion in Pakistan* (New York: Syracuse University Press, 1986), pp. 21-47.

Ali, Chaudhuri, Muhammad, *The Emergence of Pakistan* (Lahore: Research Society of Pakistan, 1986).

Amin, S.H., *Islamic Law and its Implications for the Modern World* (Glasgow: Rosyston Ltd.,1989).

Butler, Robert A., and Chagathai, M. Ikram, *Trying to Respond* (Lahore: Pakistan Jesuit Society, 1994).

Dharmaraja, Jacob, *Colonialism and Christian Mission: Post-Colonial Reflections* (New Delhi: ISPCK, 1993).

Doi, Rahman A., *Non-Muslims Under Shari'ah* (Lahore: Kazi Publications, 1981).

Enayat, Hamid, *Modern Islamic Political Thought* (London: Macmillan, 1982).

Fazl-ud-din, Joshua, *The Future of Christians in Pakistan* (Lahore: Punjabi Darbar Publishing House, 1949).

Geaves, R., Gabriel, T., Haddad, Y., Smith, J. (eds), *Islam and the West Post 9/11* (Aldershot: Ashgate, 2004).

Geijebels, M., 'Pakistan, Islamisation and the Christian Community', in *Al-Mushir*, 22/3 (1980), 99-109.

Ghazali, Abdus Sattar, *Pakistan: Illusions and Reality* (Islamabad: National Book Club, 1996).

Ghazi, Mahmud A., 'The law of Tahiri-I-Risalat: A social, political and historical perspective', in Tarik Jan (ed.), *Pakistan between Secularism and Islam: Ideology, Issues and Conflict* (Islamabad: Institute of Policy Studies, 1998).

Ghazzali, Abdul Sattar, *Islamic Pakistan: Illusion and Reality* (Islamabad: National Book Club, 1996).

Iqbal, Afzal, *Islamisation of Pakistan* (Delhi: Idarah-I Adabaiyat-I, 1984).

Jan, Tarik (ed.), *Pakistan between secularism and Islam: Ideology, Issues and Conflict* (Islamabad: Institute of Policy Studies, 1998).

Jan, Tarik, 'Questioning the Blasphemy Laws', in Jan, Tarik (ed.), *Pakistan between Secularism and Islam: Ideology, Issues and Conflict* (Islamabad: Institute of Policy Studies, 1998), pp. 241-56.

Kennedy, C.H. (ed.), *Pakistan 2000* (Colorado: Westview Press, 1998).

Kennedy, Charles, *Pakistan 1997* (Colorado: Westview Press, 1998).

Kymlica, Will, *Politics in the Vernacular, Nationalism, Multiculturalism and Citizenship* (Oxford: Oxford University Press, 2001).

Malik, Hafeez, *Pakistan, Founders' Aspirations and Today's Realities* (Oxford: Oxford University Press, 2001).

Malik, Iftikhar H., *Islam, Nationalism and the West: Issues of Identity in Pakistan* (London: Macmillan, 1999).

Miall, Hugh (ed.), *Minority Rights in Europe* (London: Pinter Publishers, 1994).

Mir, Amir, *The True Face of Jehadis* (Lahore: Mashal Books, 2004).

Modood, Tariq (ed.), *Church, State and Religious Minorities* (London: Policy Studies Institute, 1997).

Moghal, Dominic, *Churches' Commission on Mission Asia Forum Conference* (9 May 2003). *http://www.geocities.com/ccom_asia_forum/documents/030509_ Asia_Day_Conference_Moghal_paper.htm.*

Musharaff, Pervez, 'Time for enlightened moderation', in *Dawa'h Highlights*, XV/5 (May-June 2004): 5-8.

Papers presented at the International Congress on Quaid I Azam, Vol. II (Islamabad: Quaid I Azam University, no date).

Pax Christi International website: http://www.paxchristi.net/members/html/asia_ pacific_overview.php?mo_id=45&mo_name=National%20Commission%20for %20Justice%20and%20Peace%20of%20Pakistan.

Peace World Wide: http://www.pww.org.pk/index.php?link=NewsDetails&mod=N ews&id=14&page=4.

Rahim, I.A., 'A critique of Pakistan's blasphemy laws', in Tarik, Jan (ed.), *Pakistan between secularism, and Islam* (Islamabad: Institute of Policy Studies, 1998), pp. 195-207.

Rahim, I.A., 'Questioning the Blasphemy Laws', in Jan, Tarik (ed.), *Pakistan between Secularism and Islam: Idolatry, Power and Conflict* (Islamabad: Institute of Policy Studies, 1998), pp. 241-56.

Raza, Rafi (ed.), *Pakistan in Perspective*, 1947-1997 (Oxford: Oxford University Press, 1997).

Rooney, John, *Into Deserts* (Rawalpindi: Christian Study Centre, 1986).

Rooney, John, *On Rocky Ground* (Rawalpindi: Christian Study Centre, 1987).

Rooney, John, *Symphony on Sands* (Rawalpindi: Christian Study Centre, 1988).

Rooney, John, *Shadows in the Dark* (Rawalpindi: Christian Study Centre, 1984).

Rooney, John, *The Hesitant Dawn* (Rawalpindi: Christian Study Centre, 1984).

Rosen, Lawrence, *The Justice of Islam* (Oxford: Oxford University Press, 2002).

Schimmel, Annemarie, *Islam in the Indian Subcontinent* (Leiden-Koln: E J Brill, 1980).

Shakir, Naeem, 'The state of religious freedom in Pakistan', in *Al-Mushir*, 45/4 (2003), pp. 109-26.

Singh, Yoginder, in 'Where the Twain shall Meet', *The South Asian.Com* (May 2005)

The British Council of Churches, *Relations with People of Other Faiths – Guidelines for Dialogue in Britain* (London: The British Council of Churches, 1983).

Thornberry, Patrick, 'International and European Standards on minority rights', in Miall, Hugh, *Minority Rights in Europe* (London: Pinter Publishers, 1994), pp. 14-21.

Walbridge, Linda, *The Christians of Pakistan* (London: Routledge-Curzon, 2003).
Young, William G., *Days of Small Things* (Rawalpindi: Christian Study Centre, 1991).

Index

Mullah Omar 6, 79, 80-81, 85
Muslim League 1, 28, 31
Muttahida Majlis Amal 5, 31, 39, 69,
    80, 108

Nehru 1, 2, 85
    Report 1
NWFP (North West Frontier Province)
    1, 6, 10

Osama bin Laden 6, 66, 79, 80, 85

Pakistan People's Party (PPP) 8, 28
Palestinian issues 45, 47, 56, 81-3, 90,
    94, 98, 104, 108-9
Panjabi Christians 22, 95
Parliament 5, 10, 19, 26, 28-9, 36, 51,
    90
Police 7, 33, 38, 46, 50, 52, 55-6, 61-3,
    65, 68-9, 76, 83, 105-6
President Bush 2, 3, 39, 79, 80-82, 84-
    5, 93, 108
President Musharaff 3, 6, 8, 9, 31, 39,
    48, 56, 61, 66, 78-9, 80, 83, 85-
    7, 95, 99, 108
Prophet Muhammad 7, 30, 59, 60, 76,
    86

Qur'an 7, 11-12, 27, 30-3, 35, 46, 48-9,
    59, 60, 62-4, 68-9, 71, 75, 84,
    89, 90, 93-4, 104-5
    Qur'anic 52, 68-9, 71

Rahim, I.A. 4, 8, 30, 67, 71, 105
Rasul Baksh (Prof.) 5, 6, 8
Religious conversion 10, 18-19, 20-21,
    25, 42, 53, 55, 93, 98
Riba (interest) 29, 43
Roman Catholic Church 8, 10, 20-22,
    54, 66, 72, 92, 95, 99,100

Bengali Catholics 22
Justice and Peace Commission 49,
    65, 100

Saudi Arabia 2, 53, 77-9, 85, 104
Secularism 35, 37-8, 41, 76, 78
Shari'a 4, 12, 29, 30, 34-5, 38, 39, 42-4,
    51, 106
    Shari'a Court 6, 7, 28-9, 51, 60, 64,
        69, 76, 79, 94
    Penalties 6, 7, 12, 13, 59, 71
Sipahi-I-Sahaba 7, 28, 62, 105
St. Thomas 9, 17-18, 23
Sufi 18, 21, 25-6, 53, 59, 63, 76-7, 104
Sultana, Raziya (Dr) 5, 6, 9

Taliban 2, 3, 5, 6, 31, 54, 66, 77-9, 80,
    82, 85
The Dawn 65, 96

Ulama 4, 5, 26, 28, 30-31, 34, 36, 43,
    51-2, 56, 68-9, 77, 87, 92, 96
United Kingdom 21, 47, 81, 85, 107
Universal Islamic Declaration of
    Human Rights 52
USA 2, 3, 6, 9, 10, 39, 54, 66, 78, 80,
    85-6, 93, 101, 107, 108

Wahabi 26, 54, 63, 76-7
    Ideals 63
    Ideology 53, 77, 103
Wahabism 53-4, 76-7, 104
Waziristan 6, 66, 85

YMCA 95

Zia ul Haqq 2-4, 27, 29, 30, 39, 42, 49,
    51, 53, 60, 67, 70, 72, 75, 77, 79,
    90-91, 104, 107-8